ALAN'S WAR

First Second

New York & London

Published by First Second
First Second is an imprint of Roaring Brook Press, a
division of Holtzbrinck Publishing Holdings Limited Partnership
175 Fifth Avenue, New York, NY 10010

Distributed in Canada by H. B. Fenn and Company Ltd.
Distributed in the United Kingdom by Macmillan Children's Books, a division of Pan Macmillan.

Originally published in France under the titles *La Guerre d'Alan 1* (2000), *La Guerre d'Alan 2* (2002),
and *La Guerre d'Alan 3* (2008) by L'Association. All rights reserved.

Layout design by L'ASSOCIATION and EMMANUEL GUIBERT

Published by arrangement with L'ASSOCIATION.

Library of Congress Cataloging-in-Publication Data

Guibert, Emmanuel.
[Guerre d'Alan. English]
Alan's war / Emmanuel Guibert. — 1st ed.
p. cm.
ISBN-13: 978-1-59643-096-9
ISBN-10: 1-59643-096-6
1. Cope, Alan Ingram, 1925-1999—Comic books, strips, etc. 2. United States. Army—Biography—Comic
books, strips, etc. 3. World War, 1939-1945—Campaigns—Europe—Comic books, strips, etc. 4. Soldiers—
United States—Biography—Comic books, strips, etc. I. Title.
D769.C66G85 2008
940.54'1273092—dc22
[B]

First Second books are available for special promotions and premiums.
For details, contact: Director of Special Markets, Holtzbrinck Publishers.

First American Edition November 2008
Printed in the United States of America

1 3 5 7 9 10 8 6 4 2

EMMANUEL GUIBERT

ALAN'S WAR

THE MEMORIES OF G.I. ALAN COPE

Translation: Kathryn Pulver

Lettering: Céline Merrien

:01

First Second

New York & London

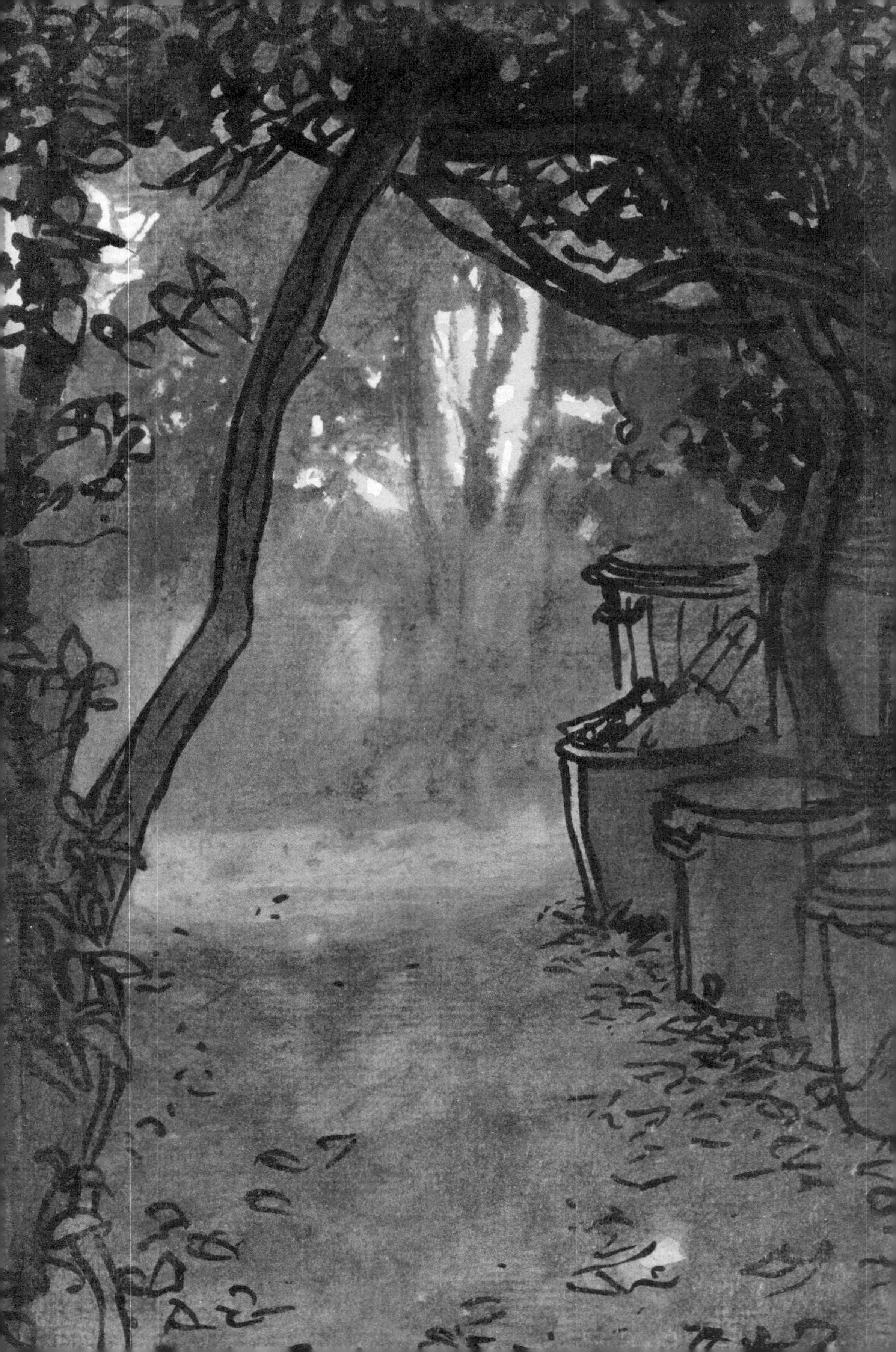

PREFACE

I met Alan Cope by chance, asking him for directions on the street. That was in June 1994. He was sixty-nine years old and I was thirty. He was living with his wife on a small island off the Atlantic coast of France, which I was visiting for the first time. Friendship was thrust upon us.

Alan was born in California in 1925, in the city of Alhambra, a suburb of Los Angeles. He had grown up in Pasadena, Altadena, and Santa Barbara and served in Europe during the Second World War. In the postwar years, he moved to France, never to return to the US. He worked as a civilian employee of the US Army, in both France and Germany, and then had moved to the island after his retirement.

One afternoon, a few days after our meeting, he started telling me stories about his experience of the war. We were walking back and forth along the ocean. He spoke well; I listened well. Save two or three, his anecdotes were nothing spectacular. They evoked only very remotely what movies or books about the Second World War had taught me. Still, I found them captivating, because of the accents of truth they contained. I could literally see what he was describing. When he stopped talking, I made him a proposal: "Let's do some books together. You'll tell me stories; I'll draw."

Alan had a garden, half a mile from his house, with a small red and white shack. That's where we started recording his account on cassette tapes. We were happy to have found a good reason to spend time together. By the end of that month of June, I already had a few hours of recordings, and a keen desire to continue. I was back by the following September. We picked up our conversations where we had left off. We'd become important to each other.

We had no idea our friendship would last only five years, but we acted as if we somehow already knew. We didn't waste the hours we spent together. We went swimming, rode bikes, tended the garden, watched movies, listened to records, played the piano, cooked, and exchanged dozens and dozens of letters, phone calls, tapes, and drawings. We conversed passionately. We never argued or lost touch.

L'ASSOCIATION, an independent comics publisher in Paris, greeted our project favorably. I started serializing pages in *Lapin*, its in-house magazine. While Alan paid close attention to my work, he also left me considerable freedom. The few mistakes he did ask me to correct were strictly of a documentary nature—a vehicle, an insignia, or the shape of a soldier's foxhole, for example. For the rest, I was free to draw his life as my imagination represented it to me. Sometimes my drawings bore only a distant resemblance to what he had lived; the setting or the people weren't true to life. He accepted it as one of the conditions for our work. At other times, he was astounded that a scene he had described to me only in general terms matched his memory of it down to the smallest detail. In all cases, he liked the result. It was that trust that allowed me to continue on my own, afterward.

Ours wasn't the work of historians. *Alan's War* is the product of the meeting of an elderly man, who had a gift for telling his life story, and a young man, who spontaneously felt compelled to write and draw it. If Alan hadn't lived through that war, I'm convinced I would still have wanted to create books with him. In fact, I intend to publish one on his childhood in California, which was probably the most intimate and beautiful part of what he confided to me. It was mostly the storyteller in him that I was drawn to—his personality, his style, his voice, and his astounding memory. That memory was not completely without flaws: readers may pick up errors or omissions here or there. As far as I can tell, they are few and far between. Although I had the chance to correct some of them, I pretty much ruled out that option. One example was that, in Chapter 3, Alan seems to have mistakenly conflated his fellow soldier Donald Carrothers with the dancer Donald O'Connor. While it appears fairly certain that those were two different people, I kept Alan's words unchanged, because it was Alan's version of events that I was trying to convey. I wanted the reader to hear what I heard—to meet the man I had met. Similarly, toward the end of book, Alan speaks discreetly of his adult life, reflecting a need for privacy that I had no intention of violating. It was the vanished world of his youth that we wanted to bring to light, not a recent or contemporary world, which would have involved living persons.

I chose the title *Alan's War* for this book to make it clear that the reader wouldn't find an essay on the life of GIs during the Second World War. It is a book about one man, Alan Cope, and what he saw, experienced, felt, and was willing to share with me, fifty years later.

I did my drawings in the same spirit. Trying to be too scrupulously exact would have constantly slowed me down in my work. So I allowed room for blank spaces and elliptical portrayals, so that my drawings too might evoke a memory.

Alan was a short man who was very tough and extremely brave, and who faced an endless string of major health problems. Even in the early days of our friendship I sometimes had to jump on a train to meet him in an emergency room. He would always resume his very active life with astonishing speed, through sheer force of will. In those trying times, we became closer than ever. In early 1998, he was diagnosed with a serious disease that transformed his existence into a battle for survival. Alan had a new war on his hands. For a year I saw him fight like a lion against an opponent that constantly pushed him further into the ropes. When he had the strength to do a recording, we spoke only of his childhood. His breath became more and more tenuous, but his stories were more essential and more lucid than ever. He continued to read our pages as they appeared in the magazine. I pulled out all the stops to allow him to see the first book come out, but I was constantly interrupting my work to spend time with him. I either brought or mailed him each new page, in which he saw himself as a young man discovering life. Following his instructions, I defended the garden against the encroaching weeds.

Alan died on August 16, 1999.

He had a running quip when he didn't want to talk about something right then and there: "I'll tell you about it in the year 2000." I'm angry at death for having cheated me out of all those conversations of 2000. I'm also angry with her for having deprived Alan of the chance to see our first book come out, in March of that year. He would've been proud to see it in the window displays of a few bookstores, and proud to read the first reviews commending our work.

But death also spared him one event that would have shaken him deeply: the destruction of his garden, his favorite place in the world, in a great storm that ravaged a large swath of Europe in December 1999. All the trees surrounding the small red and white shack were knocked down by the wind. The following spring, I saw the garden again. It had become a flat expanse of earth, leveled by bulldozers. At the time of our conversations, it was labyrinthine, dense and seemingly endless. That day, I crossed it in twenty short steps.

Magic had moved to another address.

Eight years later, I am reaching the end of the first part of my work: the war is over. As my work advanced, I felt the need, probably because I miss Alan, to tie my personal history ever more closely to his. Shortly before his death, he had encouraged me to travel to California in the year of my fortieth birthday, to pass on his greetings to General Sherman, the greatest sequoia of Sequoia National Park. I did it. I had with me pictures from the 1930s that he bequeathed to me, and I roamed the streets of Pasadena and Altadena seeking out the houses of his childhood.

I found some of them, as well as the schools he attended and the church where he sang. I identified a number of trees that he liked to climb. That was how we briefly met up again, across time.

Later on, I went to Germany, visiting the places he had occupied as a corporal in General Patton's Third Army. I found people he had known sixty years earlier and, in Alan's name, we became friends. That's why readers can find, toward the end of this book, pages that are better documented than at the beginning.

I have long dreamed of this American edition. Alan was a man on whom life had left many scars. He had a complex relationship with America— a kind of open wound. As early as 1995, I had brought up the possibility of our traveling there together. He had replied curtly, "If you want to see America, watch some TV series." He didn't want to go back to his country, that he had seen for the last time in 1948. Yet I could hear such nostalgia in his voice when he brought up what Santa Barbara was like before the war, surrounded by lemon trees, or sang his mother's favorite Steven Foster song, *Jeanie with the Light Brown Hair*.

His return to his home country is therefore happening in the form of this book. Even though Alan gave me his testimony in French— a remarkably correct and nuanced French—I have the feeling that, today, he is returning to the fold of his mother tongue.

So we are taking that trip to America together, after all.

Emmanuel Guibert
December 2007

Alan wanted this book to be dedicated to the memory of his grandmother, Ione Ingram.

I dedicate it to my parents, Jean and Jacqueline.

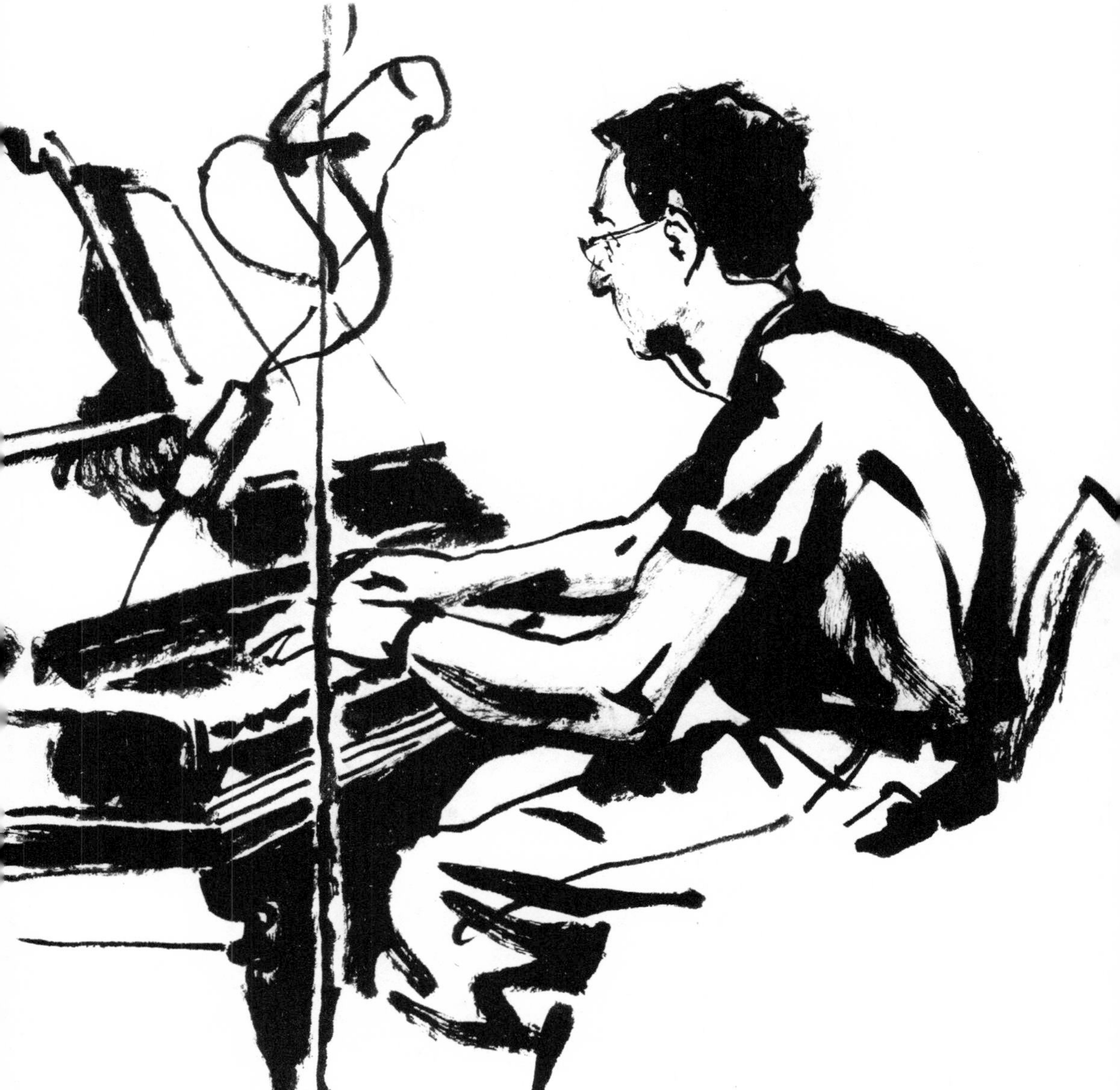

When I turned eighteen,
Uncle Sam said
he'd like me to put on a uniform
and go fight a guy by the name of Adolf.
So I did.

Alan Ingram Cope

1

I remember the day that Pearl Harbor was bombed.
I was very young, and I was delivering papers in Pasadena, California.

It was early in the morning, in the suburbs. I'd throw the paper onto the stoops in front of the houses.

Most people were still asleep, but some of them came out right away to read the headlines.

There was only one.

PEARL HARBOR BOMBED BY JAPS

I remember the looks of total surprise and shock on people's faces.

I had no idea what Pearl Harbor was. I never had time to read the paper before delivering it.

At the age of 18, like all young Americans, I was drafted.

I took some exams.
I got a perfect score on the radio operator aptitude test.

And then they put us on a train.

We're going to Fort Knox, Kentucky.

We'd only been soldiers for a day and hadn't learned anything yet, except how to make our beds. As it happens, we were put in sleeping cars—two men per bed.

Two of the young men appeared to be lovers. One of them was very shy. He was crying.

His assigned bedfellow was huge, a really, really fat man, fairly unattractive, and he was crying because he was going to have to spend the night with that guy.

His buddy said to me:

You don't know anyone here?

No, no one.

Would you mind switching with him? Look at the guy; he's about to have a nervous breakdown.

He looked so upset. I glanced at the fat man and thought, "Well, he is pretty unappealing, but..."

Okay, I'll switch.

The kid was really happy: The two of them slept together, and I shared a bed with the fat guy.

He took up most of the bed, but he couldn't help it. He was nice, actually.

That's my first memory of that trip.

It was March, and we were already
wearing our summer uniforms.
It was hot in the train, and
we had to open the windows.

Steam engines burned massive amounts
of coal, sending up great clouds of soot.
Everyone was black with it.

Very unpleasant.

And then we arrived at the Chicago freight yards.

All of a sudden they unhooked our car, and our commander told us:

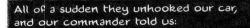

I'm leaving with the rest of the train. Another train will be coming along to take you to Fort Knox. Wait for it. You're not allowed to leave this car.

But nothing happened.
Hours went by.
We were getting hungry.

I think I see some buildings over there, maybe a street. We could cross the tracks and find a grocery store or something. Who wants to come with me?

Five of us went along.

We had to be very careful. Locomotives charged in at top speed from every direction. Because of the switching, we couldn't tell what track they were coming in on.

You'd think a train would be arriving on one track, and then suddenly it would switch to another. It was really dangerous.

We finally got out of there.

We did find a tiny neighborhood grocery store and bought bread, cookies, peanut butter, and fruit.

With everything packed in brown paper bags, we headed back.

On the way there we had been careful to get our bearings using towers and various other thingamajigs as landmarks, so we'd be able to find our way back to our rail car.

It was still just as dangerous, but we didn't get lost. We returned to the right spot.

The car was gone.

What are we going to do?

I have hardly any money.

Me neither.

We'll get in trouble.

We should walk to the station—fast. We need to get to Fort Knox as soon as possible to prove we haven't deserted, because they're going to think we've gone AWOL.

We all agreed and headed over to a freight office. When we told the agent what had happened, he laughed.

I'll send a message to the stationmaster in charge of trains coming from the West Coast.

He wrote with an electric pen that I found fascinating. He sent messages by writing on a surface that looked like paper, and at the other end, at the station, what he wrote was reproduced instantly. I'd never seen anything like it.

Anyway, an answer came through the same system: we had to leave right away.

Once we got to the station, we called Fort Knox headquarters. We had already been reported missing.

The army took care of the tickets to Louisville, via New York. Louisville is a big city near Fort Knox. The locals pronounce it "Loowavul."

It was afternoon when we pulled into Grand Central Terminal, in New York. It was my first time there.

The train to Louisville wasn't leaving until that evening, and since we were sure we'd be thrown in jail as soon as we got there, we decided to have a good time.

We climbed 102 floors to the top of the Empire State Building.

We ate for free at a servicemen's club and went to Rockefeller Center to hear a jazz band.

And then it was time to take the night train.

In the morning, when we reached Louisville, an army truck picked us up and took us to Fort Knox.

Fort Knox was a real city. 100,000 people lived there at the time. It took us a good half hour to get from the fort's entrance to our barracks.

We were warmly welcomed. No dressing down or punishment. We got our gear, like everybody else, and that was that.

2

We learned how to be soldiers.

I ended up on a tank crew.
We had a three-month training period,
because tanks were a new thing and
we had a lot to learn.

The guys in infantry only had a few
weeks' training before they were
sent off to get killed.

The first day, all draftees had to undergo
a psychological evaluation.
A serviceman would ask you questions,
some of them quite embarrassing.

Then we had to take an IQ test.
That, I did well on.
I got 132.

Now that I'm older,
I probably wouldn't fare so well.

And then the intense training began.
There were marches and obstacle courses.
We learned about all kinds of weapons,
how to behave, how to go on patrol.
We learned about condoms,
and to watch out for whores
(they didn't talk about penicillin;
at the time I'd never even heard of it).
In short, we were taught anything and everything,
even how to clean floors.
It was very thorough.

Sometimes we had to crawl under barbed wire while they shot over our heads with real bullets. If we'd stood up, we would've been killed.

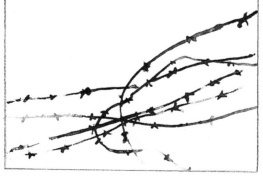

We had village combat practice. Sharpshooters hid around corners and shot at us, also with real bullets, just missing. We could see the bullet holes in the walls right next to where we were standing, and we learned to take things very seriously.

On the same day we took the village, there was an exercise that made me livid.

It happened just as we were coming out from some woods.

We stood by the side of the road, with tanks rolling by. Holes big enough for a person to fit in had been dug in the road.

You had to throw yourself in front of a tank, pick a hole, and jump into it, and then one of the tank's treads would roll right over you.

We did that, 10 or 12 of us at a time, with our rifles, but we didn't all go at once.
It was a staggered exercise.

I was the final one to get the signal to run.

I jumped into the last hole.
DAMN! IT WASN'T DEEP ENOUGH!

25

The walls of the hole had crumbled, maybe that very day. It was eight inches too shallow. I could squeeze myself in there, but I couldn't get my weapon in.

Of course, if I'd been smarter, I could've thrown it to the side or something, but I had very little time to think. The tank was bearing down on me.

"The tread is going to snap my rifle in two," I thought, "and if it breaks the wrong way, it's going to skewer me."

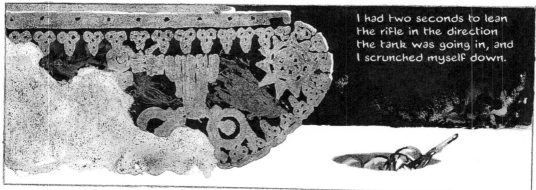

I had two seconds to lean the rifle in the direction the tank was going in, and I scrunched myself down.

Over the deafening noise of the tread passing overhead, I heard the rifle snap.

I hunkered down as far as possible, hoping it wouldn't break into my body.

It worked.

When I got out of the hole, the sergeant was furious. He wouldn't listen to a thing I said.

I didn't dare call him an asshole.

It was a dreadful experience.

3

I was part of a battalion.
There were four companies in it,
and 60 soldiers per company.

There was this one exercise where each of us had to run a relay while carrying a guy of about the same weight on our shoulders.

The companies were all mixed up, and I looked around for a guy about my size.

Can we do that?

Sure.

That's how I met Lou.

It's easy to carry someone on your shoulders. If you do it right, you can even carry men that are heavier than you. You just have to watch out that you don't crush the guy's balls.

We both had a lot of fun doing it, and we soon got to know each other.

He was totally different from me. I was kind of a shy kid. I wasn't a scaredy-cat, but I was shy, not given to athletics except for swimming and climbing trees.

Lou, on the other hand, was the kind of kid who was on the basketball team, the football team, you name it.

You never know exactly why you hit it off with someone, but we really, really did. So much so that some people thought we had certain tendencies. So Lou, who had a quick temper, ended up breaking a few noses. Haha!

We went on long marches, 20 or 30 miles, often in the boiling heat. I loved it.

One truck drove ahead of the troops, and another one stayed behind us. The front truck carried the "lister bag," the rest-stop water supply.

The other truck picked up the guys who fainted.

Rest stops lasted 15 minutes. We'd sit under a tree, have a drink, smoke a cigarette.

Often, Lou, who was in a company behind ours, would run up to meet me, and we'd have a drink together.

When we got back from marching, we were technically off duty. All the other soldiers would go to bed, exhausted. We'd say:

Well, let's go skating.

And that's what we did. It annoyed everybody.

There was a kid from another company whose name was Donald Carrothers.

He always called me "California."

Hi, California! How're ya doin'?

He was a blond farmer type, with a small, sharp nose and a look in his eyes that stayed in your memory. He wasn't very tall, but lean, with powerful thighs.

What I had noticed in particular about him is that although he was a pretty athletic guy, he had to walk bent over, because his pack was heavy and he had a small chest.

Okay, California?

I liked the way he called me "California." Sometimes we'd talk for a while. We were drawn to each other, toward a friendship that never had a chance to develop.

I'll jump forward in time now, twice, to tell you what happened to him.

Sometime around the end of the war, in May of '45, while I was in Czechoslovakia, I received two letters— a rare event. One of them was from Donald Carrothers.

Of course, it started off, "Hi, California!" and continued on:

I'VE BEEN DISCHARGED. I'M EARNING A GOOD LIVING DANCING IN CABARETS AND NIGHTCLUBS, AND I'D LIKE YOU TO COME JOIN ME AS SOON AS POSSIBLE. I NEED A PARTNER. I'LL TEACH YOU HOW TO DANCE. I KNOW YOU'LL MAKE A GREAT DANCER, AND IT'LL BE FANTASTIC.

I was totally taken aback. I hadn't heard a word from him since late '43. Truth be told, I'd forgotten all about him.

So I said no. I was very polite about it. I wrote:

IT'S AN AMAZING OFFER, AND I'M HONORED, REALLY. BUT I'M NOT SURE IT'S MY KIND OF THING. I DON'T THINK I SHOULD DO IT.

(Though I had no idea yet what it was I wanted to do.)

You know, maybe I would've been a good dancer. He probably figured that from watching me go on all those long marches with a spring in my step.

I'm going to fast-forward again, this time even further, to 1976. By then I had retired and was watching a Gene Kelly movie.

He often danced with a sidekick, Donald O'Connor.

Well, O'Connor was none other than Carrothers. I'm almost sure it was him.

I think he's dead now.

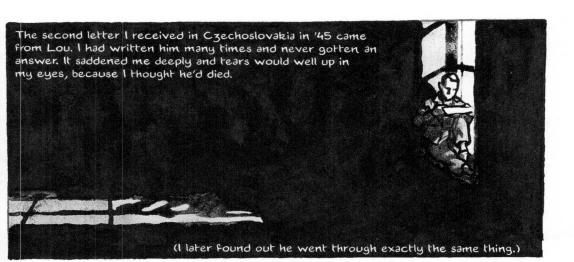

The second letter I received in Czechoslovakia in '45 came from Lou. I had written him many times and never gotten an answer. It saddened me deeply and tears would well up in my eyes, because I thought he'd died.

(I later found out he went through exactly the same thing.)

The army did its best to get letters delivered, but it was, after all, wartime. For instance, a relative had sent me a huge fruitcake...

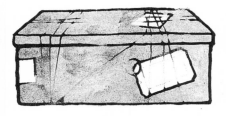

Months later, the package came back to her totally smashed, the whole thing rotten.

The truck must've been bombed or hit a mine.

Maybe it's a bit weird to say this, but, all in all, the day I got that letter from Lou was probably the best day of my life.
Even better than the day my sons were born.
To think someone's dead and then find out they're not... It's an amazing thing.
It was wonderful to think that he was alive and could write me a letter.

We'll talk about Lou some more later on.

4

I haven't told you my crabs story yet, have I?
I can tell it now.
I didn't know what crabs were, and one day,
during basic training, I got them.

I can tell you for
sure I didn't get
them in town.
I hadn't even gone
there.
I'd probably picked
them up in the
latrines.

I had a bad case of
them; it was seriously
unpleasant.

Every morning, at roll call, once he had
finished making his announcements,
our company's sergeant asked us:

> Does anyone need to go on
> sick call?

A few soldiers would fall out and go stand
next to him. He'd send everyone else off
to have breakfast and then ask each one:

> What's the matter?

I explained what was happening to me.

> They're
> called crabs.

"Crabs" is
slang for
"pubic lice;"
that's their
real name.

I don't know if you've ever seen any, but they're tiny. They wrap themselves around the root of each pubic hair, grabbing on tight with their little legs. It really hurts. If you ever get a look at one, you'll see that it looks just like a real tiny crab.

Kind of like this.

The sergeant got mad at me. He probably thought I'd done something stupid. Back then they tried really hard to keep the boys away from prostitutes.

I had no idea what to do.
Later I found out that there are ointments to kill the little things, but the sergeant didn't send me to the doctor.
He said:

Here's what you're going to do. You're going to get in the shower, slather on some shaving cream, and then use your razor until there's not a single hair left on your penis or balls, or anywhere else around there—until there's no hair left at all. Got it?

And be careful that everything goes down the drain; you can't leave any of it lying around. You'll see; they'll all be gone.

I have to admit, it does work.

Still—he was a real bastard, because, as you can imagine, it was a difficult and unpleasant business.

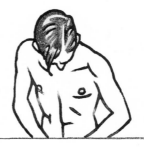

But that wasn't the end of it...

The thing about hair is that it grows back. In the beginning it's really short and chafes like crazy.

To make things worse, we were always walking, exercising, doing sports, and so on.
I bought talc, of course, and I protected myself as best I could, but I suffered a lot.

After that I was careful.

I didn't want to catch them again.
The toilets weren't in separate stalls.

They were lined up against the wall in groups of six or seven.

The lack of privacy was hard.

Shortly after the crabs episode, there was an accident.

The army brought in workmen to fix the heating system.

They piped the hot water into the latrines.

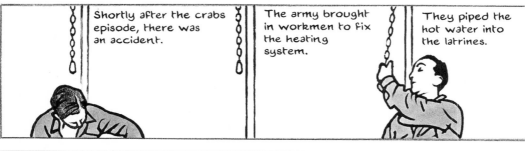

The next morning, all the guys who flushed sitting down got badly burned.

Luckily, I wasn't one of them.

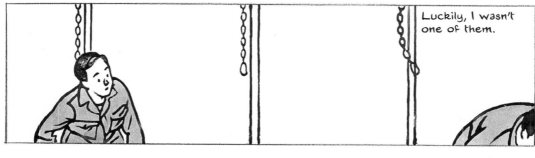

5

My father hadn't taught me how to drive,
probably because my stepmother was against it.
Otherwise he would've taught me.
He was a really nice guy.
At 18, I only knew how to ride a bike.
So the first motor vehicle I ever learned to drive was a tank.

They're pretty nasty machines,
I have to say.
When the ground is dry—and in
Kentucky the soil is clay—
they churn up an unbelievable
amount of dust.

And when it rains, it's really no fun.
Everything turns to mud,
and then, to top it all off,
you have to clean the tank
when training's over for the day.

The most important thing is to get the mud off each tread link. You can use a small stick, a tree branch, anything you can find. The mud is sticky and almost impossible to remove.

Back then, tank engines were aircraft engines, the radial kind, like on old propeller planes. They were called radial because they had a circular shape, with spark plugs around the outside. They gobbled an unbelievable amount of fuel.

We had jerry cans, and we learned— even me, little Cope—to carry up to four of them at a time, two in each hand. They were really, really heavy.

I don't know if you've heard anything about driving those tanks...
You had two treads, but no steering wheel. So first of all, you needed to get the thing started. That wasn't too hard. You turned the key and if the thing was working, the motor started up.

You were uncomfortably seated and couldn't see much of anything. If you closed the hatch, all you had to look through was a kind of slit.

(That's why when we were in town and not in the middle of combat, a soldier always walked ahead of the tank to direct it.)

There was an accelerator and a braking system. To steer, you had to mechanically brake one of the treads by pulling on a handle that looked like a plane's stick. So one tread slowed down while the other kept going at the speed set by the accelerator, and that made the tank turn.

To turn right, you'd pull on the right handle, the right tread would slow, and you'd go right.

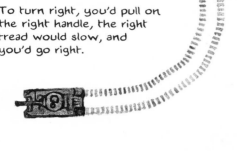

If you pulled hard, the tread would come to a complete stop, and then you'd make a really sharp turn.

To stop the tank, you just pulled on both handles.

There was also a kind of clutch, but nothing like a car's clutch. It allowed the engine to run without the tank moving forward.

The tanks were built to hold four people: the driver, in the hull on the left; the radio operator, in the hull on the right; and the tank commander and the gunner, in the turret. The gunner became the commander if the commander was killed or wounded.

The turret usually had a rail around it with a big, roller-mounted machine gun on top, a .50 caliber, so you couldn't close the turret. You had to stand up in it. When it was cold, you'd put a towel between the two parts of your helmet to make a kind of shawl. When it rained—well, it rained.

The four of them communicated using headphones and a small microphone.
As I already told you, the driver couldn't see much and neither could the radio operator.
If the gunner went back to his seat, the commander was
the only one who could really see what was happening.

He'd direct the maneuvers and firing, using a system based on a clock face: target at 3 o'clock, at 10 o'clock, and so on. He'd also give distances, so when the gunner, peering through a small window, eventually got a visual, he could fire. Today, it's probably all done electronically, but for us, it was a matter of guesswork. Good-quality guesswork.

So, like everyone else, I learned how to drive this thing. It was kind of fun. In the beginning, it wasn't particularly easy. The training lasted at least two weeks, and toward the end they let us knock down some trees. They were oaks of some kind, not too thick but very tall.

There were three of us in the tank: the instructor, who sat in the radio operator's seat, and two trainees taking turns in the commander's seat and in the turret.

I was the first driver and did a good job knocking over my trees. I got a very good grade.

Then I switched places with the other guy and ended up alone in the turret, in the gunner's seat.

The tank was heading straight for a big tree.

Instead of falling over in one piece when it was hit, the tree, which was probably not very healthy, snapped in the middle.

The bottom half landed in front of the tank.

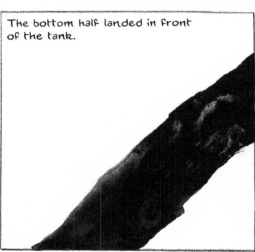

The top part fell right into the turret.

Luckily, the tree landed
next to me and not on my head,
or I would've been dead.
If there'd been two of us, one of us
would've been killed for sure.
It scared me, and the instructor too.
It didn't hurt the tank,
but it damaged
the turret seats.

It's strange—throughout
that time and later, during
the war itself, I constantly
had dangerous things
happen to me that weren't
combat related.

6

We would spend the whole day learning how to maneuver and maintain a tank, and we were exhausted.
Luckily, Lou's company was getting the same training.
We'd meet up at night and talk for a while.
We slept in army tents, pretty uncomfortably, far from the fort, in the middle of nowhere.

Lou would say:

Come on, let's go steal something to eat.

He'd sneak into his company's mess tent (he was a bit of a daredevil), and he'd steal bread, butter, and onions.
He loved raw onions.

We'd make huge bread, butter, and onion sandwiches. They're fairly hard to digest, but tasty.

Since that time, I've always liked that kind of sandwich.

And then we were given Saturday afternoon and Sunday off to go back to the fort, which everybody did, and Lou got really depressed.

I'm sick of all this, I'm sick of the army. It's pointless. I'm just gonna go AWOL.

When the trucks that were taking everybody back left, on Sunday at around 4 o'clock, he hid, and I stayed with him.

I said:

I'm staying with you, but I'm not deserting. I'll pin you down if I have to—you can't do this.

I HATE those tanks!

In the movies you always see them on fire with the guys inside frying. I LOATHE THEM!

I don't like the thought of being burned alive in a tank. At night I dream that I'm frying in one, like in the movies.

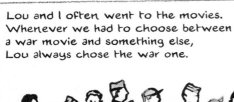

Lou and I often went to the movies. Whenever we had to choose between a war movie and something else, Lou always chose the war one.

I didn't necessarily identify with the actors.

Lou, why do we have to see another war movie?

Because I wonder how I'll react in those situations.

He was very brave and very tough, but I guess he was afraid of reacting badly during combat.

Listen, to tell you the truth, I hate tanks too. What I hate is cleaning them.

AH! You see?

I hadn't really thought about it, but now that you mention burning up in a tank, I have to admit I don't like the idea either.

Okay! So?

We can't go AWOL.

It took me six hours to convince him.

It was about 10:30 p.m. when I said:

You're coming back with me.

Okay.

We're going to have to walk all the way there.

Yeah, yeah, okay.

You know the way, Alan?

Of course.

We both started walking. It took hours. We were completely exhausted by the time we got back to our companies.

The next day, he said:

You know what I'm going to do? I'm going to volunteer to join the paratroopers. What do you think? You could, too.

It might be more dangerous than tanks, but the idea of fighting as a paratrooper doesn't scare me. Frying inside a tank, now that does.

I agreed.

We went over to headquarters.

It can't hurt to ask. We'll see what happens.

So we went ahead and asked. We had to take another physical and an aptitude test, which we passed.

We got our answer.

They turned down our request because there was a freeze on all transfers. Our training was almost over, and headquarters had already decided how each soldier was going to be used.

I think I would've enjoyed being a paratrooper, but maybe I wouldn't be here today to talk about it.

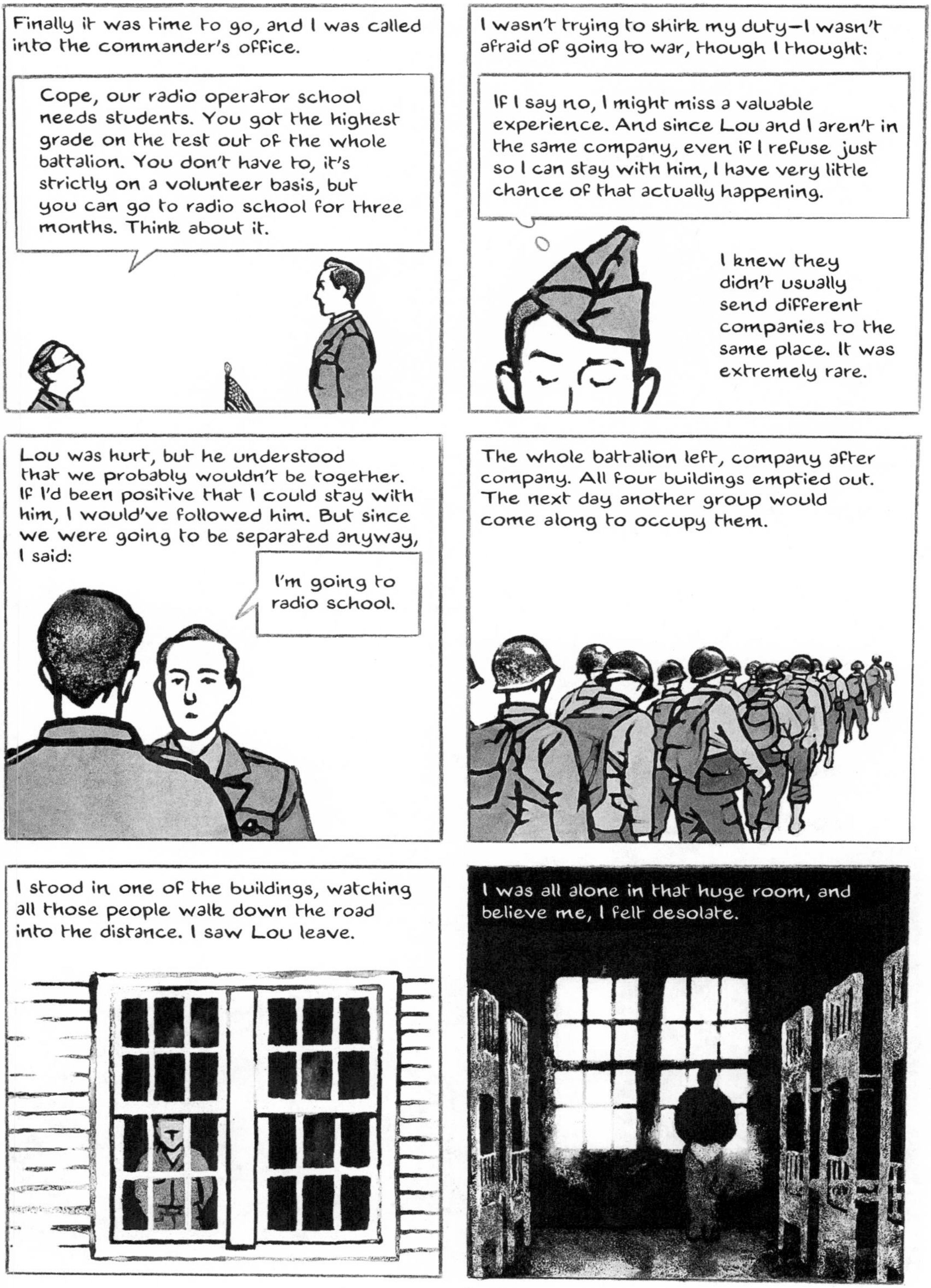
Finally it was time to go, and I was called into the commander's office.
Cope, our radio operator school needs students. You got the highest grade on the test out of the whole battalion. You don't have to, it's strictly on a volunteer basis, but you can go to radio school for three months. Think about it.
I wasn't trying to shirk my duty—I wasn't afraid of going to war, though I thought:
If I say no, I might miss a valuable experience. And since Lou and I aren't in the same company, even if I refuse just so I can stay with him, I have very little chance of that actually happening.
I knew they didn't usually send different companies to the same place. It was extremely rare.
Lou was hurt, but he understood that we probably wouldn't be together. If I'd been positive that I could stay with him, I would've followed him. But since we were going to be separated anyway, I said:
I'm going to radio school.
The whole battalion left, company after company. All four buildings emptied out. The next day another group would come along to occupy them.
I stood in one of the buildings, watching all those people walk down the road into the distance. I saw Lou leave.
I was all alone in that huge room, and believe me, I felt desolate.

7

Okay, so now I was learning to be a radio operator.

It was great training and lasted three months.

We spent several hours a day

sending and receiving messages.

Some guys practically had nervous

breakdowns trying to learn the code.

We also learned cryptography, the basics of radio operation, transmission procedures (along with the long list of international Q codes, which consist of the letter Q followed by a few other letters, usually two), how to handle a radio, transmitting using voice codes, and more...

Toward the end of the three months of training, we learned how to operate a radio under combat conditions.

They put us in half-tracks and took us down unbelievably bad roads and onto riverbeds, where we were in constant danger of overturning.

You'd strap the transmitter to your thigh, and you had to send messages.

Outside, huge loudspeakers blared combat sounds—planes zooming, bombs exploding, people screaming.

In the midst of it all, you still had to be able to hear and transcribe.

I became a good medium-speed radio operator. I placed first in a class of 300.

They soon asked me to become an instructor. Remember, I was still just a regular private—not even first class.

I liked the idea.

I taught international Morse code to privates and sometimes to noncommissioned officers.
You had to determine their strengths and weaknesses and figure out why they did certain things wrong.
It was pretty interesting.

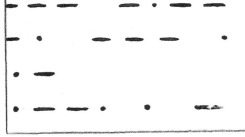

But the most enjoyable part was cryptography. At the time we had a wonderful little machine that encrypted and decrypted messages.
A secret machine.

It was a little over five inches long, slightly less than that in width, and almost three inches high. It had levers and disks. I don't remember how it worked anymore.

Maybe I forgot how because, like a good keeper of secrets, I was supposed to.

I had learned everything there was to know about that little machine. In the mornings I'd teach 100 people at a time to use it, including some high-ranking officers, even colonels.

You occasionally had to correct them. Truth be told, older guys like that sometimes take a lot longer to learn new stuff than younger ones do, don't you think?

In the afternoons I went back to the half-tracks, this time as an instructor, with four or five operators at a time. I made a few friends among those students.

I remember two really great guys. They had girlfriends in Louisville and all they thought about was getting laid.

Every 20 minutes or so, I'd have to bring them back to the harsh reality of radio operation. They were really nice guys, but real goofballs.

I bunked with other instructors. One day, to make fun of me, they played a dirty trick.

There was going to be an inspection. A sign had been posted on the notice board saying that everyone had to be out of the barracks by, let's say, 7 a.m. I didn't see it.

I had stayed out very late the night before, as I had the next morning off. The other guys let me sleep.

The commander showed up with a friend of his he had invited to inspect our barracks, and they found me there, snoring away.

My punishment was that I couldn't go out for a week. I was confined to the school, mess hall, and barracks.

So I made a dummy, a very realistic dummy. I put it in my bed and went out every single night. It was my way of saying "up yours."

So while war raged all over the world, there I was, peacefully studying and teaching radio. I didn't feel guilty, though. I did think about it, of course, but basically, I was just doing my job.

8

Now let me tell you about a turning point in my life.
Fort Knox had two big rec halls for its soldiers,
which were run by the army recreation service.
They were huge places where you could play cards, watch movies,
get coffee—with milk and sugar if you wanted.
I think they even handed out a few cigarettes and doughnuts.
It was nice.

One evening, in one of those halls,
I happened to climb a small flight of stairs
and found myself in front of a door—a
plain, nondescript door.

I opened it.

Suddenly there were only five or six people, not 500. The walls were soundproof. You couldn't hear any of the hubbub outside.

There was a piano, really comfortable leather chairs, nice curtains, and, most important, an excellent record player, the very latest thing at the time, which played 78 rpm disks.

The record collection was impressive.

I later learned that it had all been put together by a group of women who wanted to do something for the troops. Needless to say, it didn't look like anything I'd seen in the army up until then.

Walking into that music room, I found myself in a world I still live in today—the world of great music.

Soon, with two or three other guys, I was running the place. Night after night I basically took charge of the room.

It wasn't that I didn't know great music existed, but hearing it this way was a revelation. Experiencing that music filled me with such joy that I could have stayed on as a radio instructor for the next 10 years.

They had Bach, Schubert, Handel, Beethoven quartets played by the original Budapest String Quartet, and many other wonderful pieces.

FRANZ SCHUBERT
STRING QUARTET IN D MINOR · D 810
A · ALLEGRO
DEATH AND THE MAIDEN

UDWIG
THOV
LIN CON

Some of the soldiers knew a lot about music and explained things to me. For instance, there was this one fairly pedantic guy who had been studying musicology before he was drafted.

Another student friend knew of a group at the University of Louisville that put on record concerts. That guy, David Diamond, had money, and if we could get leave at the same time, he'd pay for a hotel room in Louisville, and we'd go to the concert.

It was a very classy operation. There were at most 20 people in an opulent living room. We listened to operas, which somebody introduced and gave commentary on. That's how I discovered <u>Don Giovanni</u>.

In the Fort Knox music room I met a radio student by the name of Amiel Philip Van Teslaar. He was charming, and brilliant. I think he had an IQ of 150— a borderline genius.

He knew that famous philosopher personally, you know... He's dead now. Very modern. Oh well, it'll come back to me.

Amiel was the descendant of a dark Dutch family, black Dutchmen.
You know, there are two kinds of Dutch people: the typical Germanic ones, and the ones whose ancestors came from Spain.
Those people were often Jewish, but they frequently had Moorish ancestry and were dark-skinned.

Amiel knew everything. Everything about music, math, literature. For instance, he'd already read all of Proust. He hated the army, of course, and he hated radio operation.

He loved the music room. He was often in such a hurry to get there that he wouldn't bother to change his clothes or eat, and his hair would be full of red dust.

Amiel, shake out your hair. It's covered in dirt.

I don't give a damn. I came here to listen to music, not wash my hair.

He knew a bit about tennis, so I got my hands on two racquets and we played.

Sometimes we'd go into town and try to drink, but we were young, and in those days you had to show your identification. If you weren't 21, you couldn't order a beer in a Louisville bar or even buy one in a store.

Once Amiel said to me:

I want some Benedictine.

I don't know how we did it, but we finally managed to convince a liquor store clerk to sell us a bottle of Benedictine.

I want ponies, too.

Ponies are tiny little stemmed glasses, very delicate ones, used for small amounts of hard liquor. We found some in a glass-ware shop.

I hid the bottle and ponies in my barracks. We took them with us when we went to play tennis.

It's nice to drink Benedictine from ponies. It wouldn't be very refined to drink it straight from the bottle.

(Despite the dirt in his hair, he was a very refined person.)

I liked Amiel a lot. We got along like a house on fire. But then I left to go to war in Europe and I lost touch with him completely.

Much later, in 1953 when my civilian post with the Air Force in Chateauroux was terminated, I went to the civilian personnel services at headquarters in Orleans to try to find another job.

I sat down in the waiting room. I looked left... I looked right, and who did I see? Haha! Amiel!

He was sitting there for the same reason I was. Except that he had all sorts of degrees and ended up finding work easily.

I, however, didn't find anything for a year. That time of my life was disastrous.

In May 1954, I ended up getting hired by the army's legal services department in La Rochelle. I didn't have a penny to my name. And who do I bump into? Amiel, again!

He had found a really good, high-paying job in La Rochelle. He was married to a Frenchwoman. He said to me:

You can come and eat dinners with us, no problem, until you start making money again.

I had a place to live, but not enough money to eat. For a while I ate only a half a baguette of bread a day.

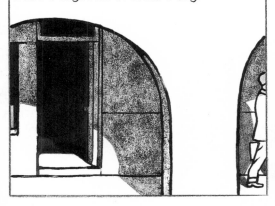

We saw each other again for a while, then lost touch for good. It was too bad, because he was a real friend. I learned 23 years later that he had become the dean of the American University of Paris.

I wrote to him, but he never answered. I don't know if he ever got my letter.

By the way, I just remembered the name of that famous philosopher: it was Bertrand Russell.

9

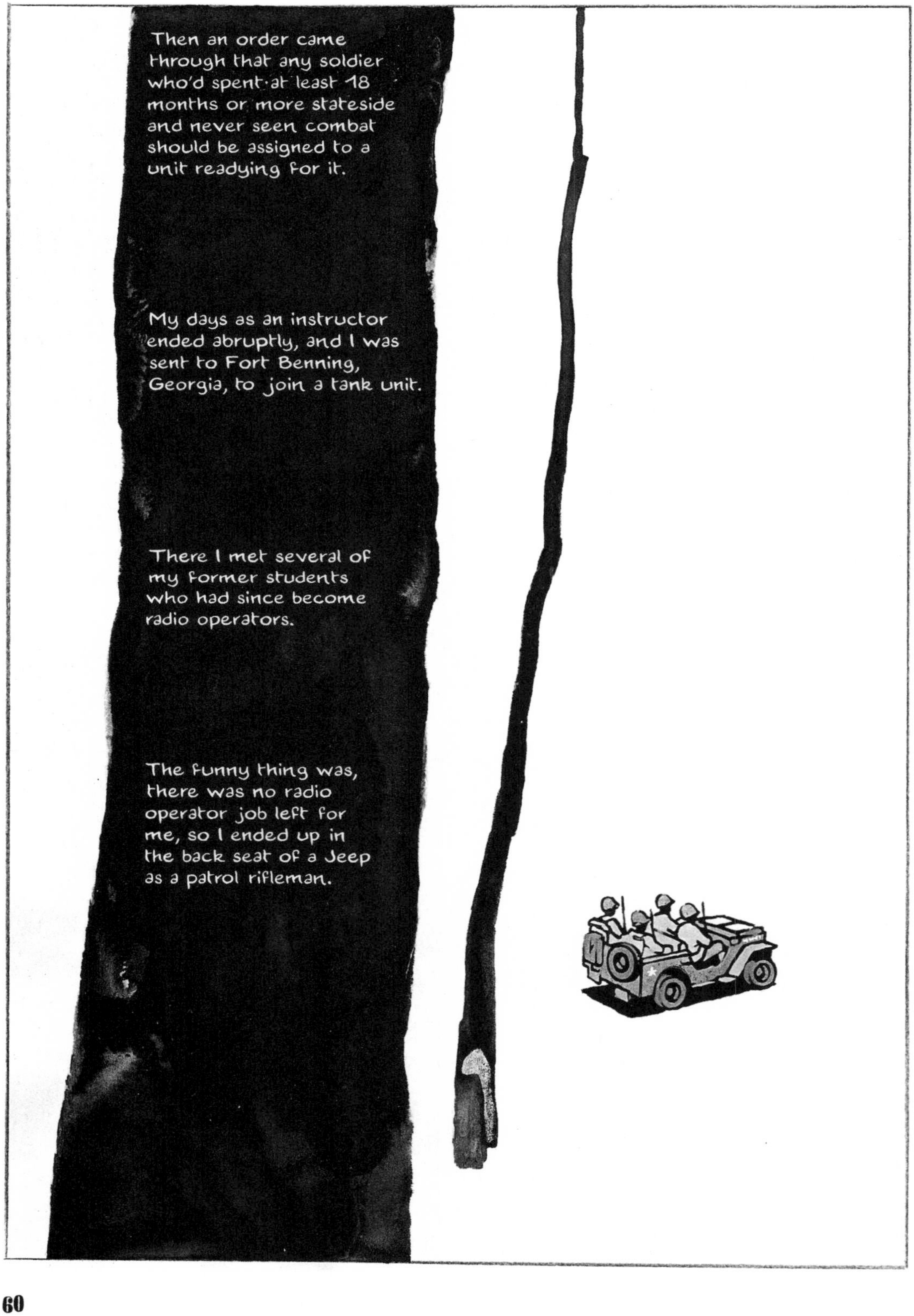
Then an order came through that any soldier who'd spent at least 18 months or more stateside and never seen combat should be assigned to a unit readying for it.
My days as an instructor ended abruptly, and I was sent to Fort Benning, Georgia, to join a tank unit.
There I met several of my former students who had since become radio operators.
The funny thing was, there was no radio operator job left for me, so I ended up in the back seat of a Jeep as a patrol rifleman.

Life wasn't fun.
It was wintertime, and very cold,
which made patrol work pretty tough.

We had to crawl all around the Jeep, two of us on the right and two on the left, checking out the sides of the road, clumps of trees, and so on. I said to myself:

Am I really going to spend the entire war crawling around like this?

Luckily, the Jeep commander, Sergeant John Marker, was a great guy. We became good friends. He said to me:

Cope, you absolutely have to learn to drive something other than a tank.

I agree! Let me drive!

So whenever we had a stretch of open road ahead of us, he'd let me drive. I learned pretty fast.

Okay, so I wasn't a great driver, but I at least knew how to shift gears and put the Jeep in four-wheel drive.

There was a real mixed bag of soldiers at Fort Benning.
Some of them were outstanding, but for the most part they weren't so great.
They were useless shirkers. Not qualified shirkers, like me, just lazy guys
who didn't know how to do a thing.

One of my fellow soldiers was a very
nice hillbilly from the Ozark mountains
who'd spent his whole life barefoot.
It hurt him to wear shoes.

I figured that maybe I could do better,
so a buddy and I asked to go to officer
training.

You could
stay there for
two years and
come out
a lieutenant.

I was interviewed by an officers' committee.
The thing is, I didn't know enough about the way the army
was organized, for the simple reason that I'd never been
interested enough to find out.

How does a division operate? What is it comprised of? What does each branch of the service do?

Overall, my answers were pretty vague.

At one point, you had to look at every officer's collar and identify his branch insignia. That I could probably have managed quite well.

But they were sitting high up, as in a courtroom, right in front of a long picture window.

All of a sudden the setting sun shined directly through the window.

I'm sorry, I can't see anything, the sun is in my eyes.

They laughed and did nothing to help me.

It turned out I wasn't officer material.

I wasn't really the military type; I was more of a dreamer.

63

10

While I was at Fort Benning, I got a letter
from Lou, who was at another camp
pretty far away.

He suggested that we try to see
each other one last time.

He'd drawn the winning lot for
a 24-hour leave, which, on a weekend,
meant almost two days.

He said in his letter:

"If you can get leave too, there's
a small town somewhere between
your camp and mine. It's just a
short bus ride away."

(I forget the name of the town,
unfortunately.)

"There's a bus leaving
Fort Benning on such and
such day at such and such time.
You'll get into town in the middle
of the afternoon.
We could rent a room, have dinner,
talk as long as we want,
and then have breakfast the next
morning before returning to camp.

Write back quickly."

He'd even taken
the trouble to check
the bus schedule for me.

I went to see the first sergeant and explained our situation. I asked him if it was possible to get 24-hour leave.
To my great surprise, he was very understanding.
You know, your buddy's really nice to set this up. I'll help you too and get you your leave—let me check the schedule.
He checked, and it was okay.
When the day came, I got on the bus, thrilled that Lou had thought of organizing this.
BUS STOP
It never would have occurred to me.
So we met up. Neither one of us was rich, but we had brought enough money to rent a very nice room in a comfortable hotel.
We talked for a long time before dinner. We told each other our life stories, what we had done, what we hadn't done, and related news of our families.
We even had a drink, something we never did. I remember we had dry martinis. They're three-fifths gin and two-fifths Noilly Prat—really good and very strong.

Of course, we also talked half the night before falling asleep.

The next day, after breakfast, we said good-bye, very glad about our friendship, and knowing that this time, we might never see each other again.

Okay. Bye, Lou.

That was just before he left the States to go to war. Oh, you would have liked him. He was a really great guy. A stand-up guy, a really strong guy. And as I've mentioned, I didn't hear from him again for a very long time.

11

In my 20 months in the service, I had been home to see my family in California only twice.

It was a 10-day round-trip by train.

The cars were absolutely packed.

The first trip was wrenching. My Cope grandfather had died while I was in basic training, and I hadn't been able to go home for his funeral. Now my grandma was dying.

She was in a gigantic Los Angeles hospital. It was so huge that its staff had to use roller skates to get around.

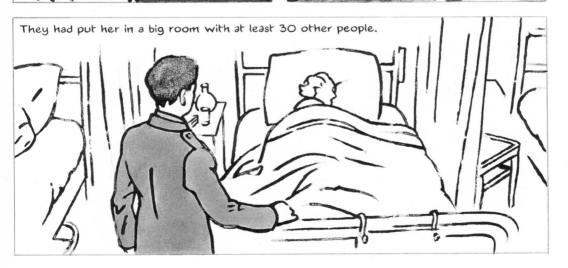

They had put her in a big room with at least 30 other people.

I had always been very close to my paternal grandmother. We really loved each other. She didn't like my stepmother, and my stepmother didn't like her, so there was no way they were going to care for her at home.

I can understand that.

I was in uniform. We weren't allowed to wear civilian clothing on leave. Of course, she was happy to see me, but she was sad, too, as dying people can be.

She made an effort to talk a bit.

You see that woman over there, near the entrance, in the very first bed?

Yes.

Well, she's a hermaphrodite.

Really?

I was surprised she even knew the word.

I'd never seen one before.

She still noticed everything around her.

She died shortly afterward. She'd had a tough life— but that's another story. I have her engagement ring, which I carry, in her memory.

My wedding ring was hers too. I had it sized for me.

That time I also saw my friend Martha, and I went out with my friend Egypt. We saw "Gone With the Wind."

My stepmother was furious.

I told you not to see that movie! It's full of swear words and people sleeping with each other!

She wasn't all that straitlaced, though. She was just weird, that's all I can say.

What are you going on about? I saw it, I liked it— that's all there is to it, so be quiet.

When I was little, I obeyed her. Later on, of course, I did nothing of the sort.

Still, we got along well, because I was a nice, well-brought-up kid, and I could see that my father was happy to have a young wife. I treated her well—better than she treated me, that's for sure.

I got lucky with my second leave, winning the draw before the major maneuvers preceding our departure for combat duty.

The first train I took I had to hail like a tram. It dropped me off at a station where I caught another train to California via the southern route.

It was a difficult trip, because it was wintertime, there was nothing to eat, and people were sleeping all over the place in corridors and baggage racks. I had a seat; that was a miracle.

There was absolutely no food service, except when we stopped at stations and vendors came around with sandwiches, Cokes, coffee, and so on. We bought things through the window.

I had a seat right by the corridor and I stayed there, except to go to the restroom. My neighbor saved it for me.

On the second to last day, as I was coming out of the toilets, I saw a guy's legs about to disappear out the window. He was jumping from the train; he was about to kill himself.

Luckily, he was very small, and I was able to grab him and pull him back in.

He was an 18-year-old sailor, and he was stone drunk. He couldn't even stand up.

I carried him back to my seat and held him on my lap all day and all night. He was unconscious the whole time.

The next morning he finally woke up.

What am I doing here?

OW! You're hurting me!

What do you mean I'm hurting you? I'm not hurting you!

Oh. It's my comb...

All that time his comb had been jabbing him in the thigh. I couldn't possibly have known.

What am I doing here with you?

You don't remember a thing?

No.

At the Los Angeles train station, I was pleased to see my father, my stepmother, Caroline, and her parents waiting for me.

I spent a few days with them. It was nice. I saw friends and I also saw a lot of the Zediker family—Egypt's family.

My stepmother's parents, who lived on the same street as Egypt—almost directly across the street—didn't like the Zedikers. They couldn't stand the notion of my hanging around with them.

None of all this was based on fact, just on the idea that they had a bad reputation.

They didn't have a bad reputation AT ALL.

Anyway, the day soon came when I had to leave. My family was supposed to take me to the station, and the Zedikers came too.

My family started sulking when they saw the Zedikers.

They hardly said good-bye to me, they were so offended that my friends had come along.

Coming from my father, that surprised me. I still don't understand it. I don't think he was diffident, but he didn't like to hurt other people's feelings, so he probably thought the best thing was just to keep quiet.

My friends hugged and kissed me a lot, my family hardly at all. Finally, only Caroline came up to the train door and kissed me once more and said good-bye.

I was deeply shocked and, because my own father was part of it, I was appalled—simply furious.

Don't worry, I didn't shed any tears, but I thought: "It's unbelievable; if your own family's affection can be so hypocritical, it isn't real."

I wrote them a letter telling them exactly how I felt, choosing my words carefully.

What's the matter with you? You have a son you're seeing for what may be the last time, a son who might get killed in the war, and the best you can do is act the way you did? I'm really disappointed in you.

I sent them each a copy. That's probably why they didn't write to me too often after I left.

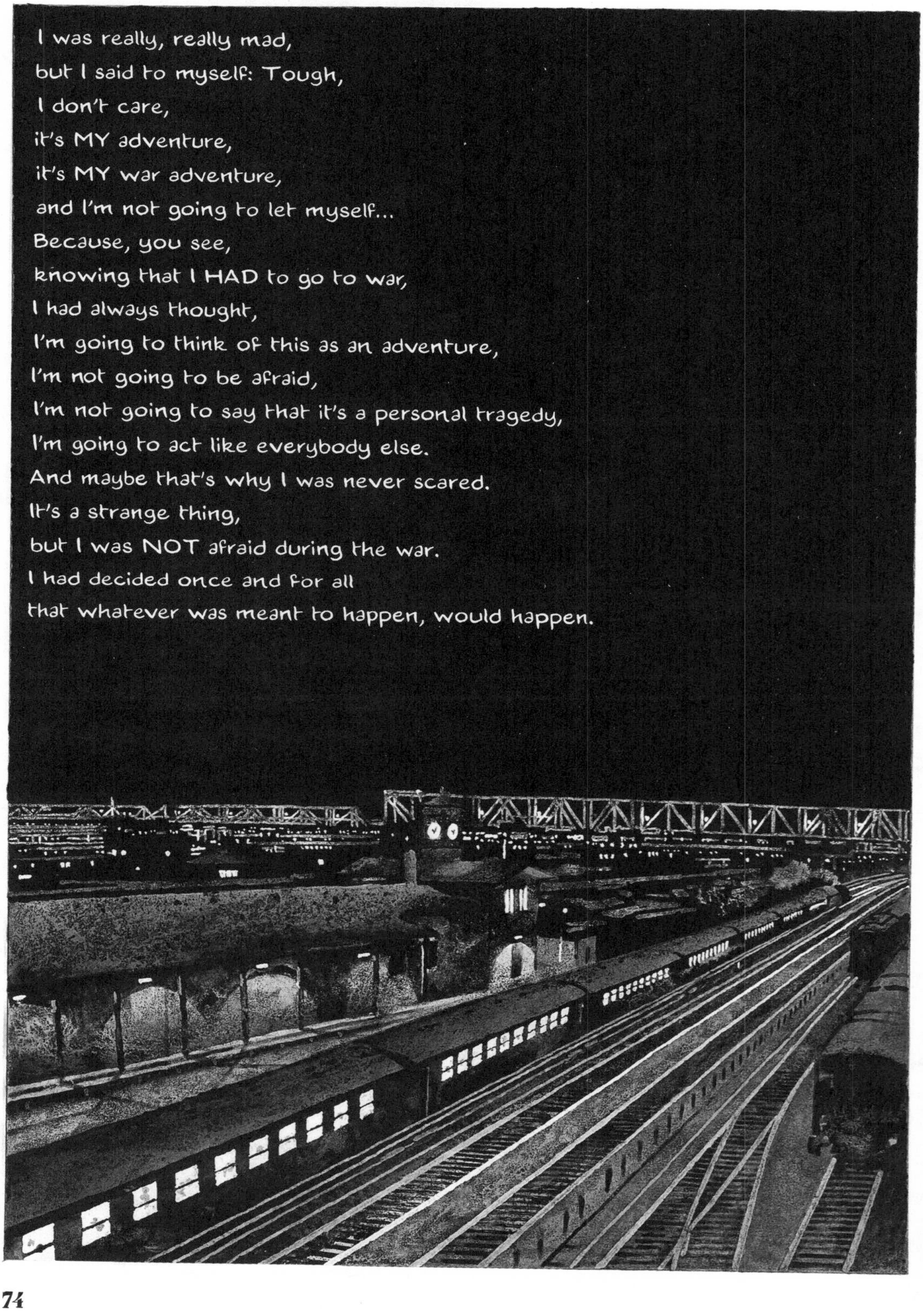
I was really, really mad,
but I said to myself: Tough,
I don't care,
it's MY adventure,
it's MY war adventure,
and I'm not going to let myself...
Because, you see,
knowing that I HAD to go to war,
I had always thought,
I'm going to think of this as an adventure,
I'm not going to be afraid,
I'm not going to say that it's a personal tragedy,
I'm going to act like everybody else.
And maybe that's why I was never scared.
It's a strange thing,
but I was NOT afraid during the war.
I had decided once and for all
that whatever was meant to happen, would happen.

12

As soon as I returned from leave, I had to go on maneuvers for two weeks.
My battalion was already there, so I set out to catch up with it, alone in the back of a supply truck.
I felt—we all felt—that we'd soon be going to war.

Earlier I had learned how to use a very special weapon. Hardly anyone was able to hit the target with it, but I could.

You took a small rifle, attached an adaptor to it, and put a kind of long grenade on top of the whole thing. It was supposed to be powerful enough to blow up a tank. It certainly worked—it was a terrible device. But the problem was firing it.

You'd sit on the ground with your legs crossed, your back hunched, and your tailbone tucked in.

You'd shoulder the rifle and hold it tightly, because the recoil was unbelievable (if you'd been standing up, it would have broken either your shoulder or your back).

There was no real system for aiming; you just had to take a guess.

PAH

We'd shoot in the air, because the thing offered so much resistance upon firing that there was no way it could follow a straight path.

The grenade flew up into the air, arced downward, and was supposed to land on the tank.

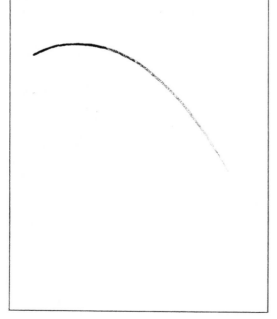

Meanwhile, the recoil was so violent it knocked us backward, we'd do a somersault, and end up sitting down again. Of course, you couldn't let go of your weapon. If you did the whole thing properly, it didn't hurt. Otherwise, there could be trouble.

When you're on maneuvers, there are always two opposing sides. I was so good with the weapon, they'd picked me to eliminate a tank that was supposed to appear suddenly from between some trees.

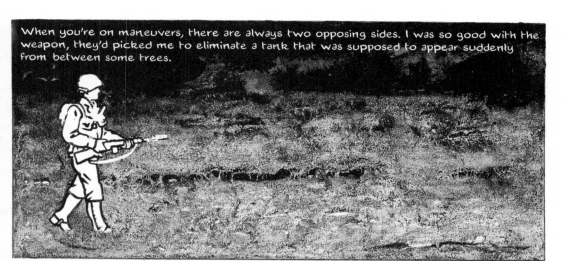

There were two reasons I stepped on an antipersonnel mine. First, although the detonating cord was pretty obvious, I was so focused on the tank's arrival that I wasn't thinking about anything else.

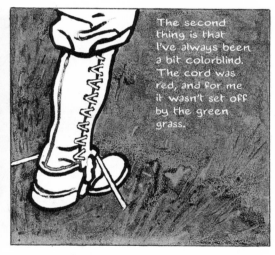

The second thing is that I've always been a bit colorblind. The cord was red, and for me it wasn't set off by the green grass.

What did get set off, however, was the fake grenade, so I was dead.

I was terribly embarrassed and tried to apologize, but that's not military-speak. The monitor was furious.

But you're dead, Cope! What are we going to do?

We could hear the tank coming. He quickly consulted another sergeant and said to me:

Okay, you're only slightly wounded. You're going to shoot anyway.

Sit down, and shoot as soon as you can see the whole tank.

I said to myself, you've absolutely got to hit it.

Well, I did. Right smack in the middle.

PAH

Of course it didn't explode, but the grenade hit the armor plating with a clunk.

And that was that.

We didn't get a lot to eat on maneuvers. I lost a lot of weight.

One evening, a soldier said:

I went for a walk in the woods last night, and I met a lumberjack who lives there in a cabin. If we go over there later on, he'll sell us a small, inexpensive meal—with a nice steak.

We never got to eat really good steak in the army. As for me, I simply had never had any. I came from a family that bought cheaper things, like ground meat. So I went along.

We walked in the woods for a good hour and did find a lumberjack's cabin. It could've been a century old.

We went into the kitchen, which was extremely rustic, and were served delicious steak and good coffee.

I think I might have paid 50 cents.

13

When we got back to the fort, preparations for our departure started in earnest.
Since we were on the east coast and in a tank unit,
we had been pretty sure for a while
that we'd be headed for Europe.

I was informed that I had been made
a gunner, replacing a guy on sick leave.

Why me?

Because your file says that you always hit the target during practice.

I was thrilled to leave the Jeep and my patrolman's job.

It was a gunner's post in an armored car,
which is used for reconnaissance. It looks
like a tank, but it's on wheels.

The cannon isn't for offensive purposes,
but it's long and pretty big. It had to be
cleaned daily, even if it hadn't been used.

More good news—the commander of my
armored car was my friend John Marker.

Listen, Cope,
before we leave
you should practice
firing the cannon.

That's true,
I've only done
simulations.

So we spent half a day on target practice.

I followed his orders, and everything went well.

The radio operator's name was Kulik. He was a New York Jew whose parents owned a delicatessen.

The driver was called Polski. He was, obviously, of Polish descent. In civilian life, he drove trucks loaded with dynamite.

I'll have a lot more to say about the two of them later on.

Finally it was time to go. We left three times. We'd get on the road but then we'd turn around before reaching any ship and return to the fort. That was the army's system for getting the troops used to stress.

The third time, we said:
"Please! Not again! If this one's real, it'll be a relief. Each time we have to pack and unpack everything."
But this time we really left.

We didn't know what port we were going to. They never told us our destination. We ended up in front of a huge cruise liner, and we went aboard.

I wasn't with Marker or the others anymore. I didn't know anyone around me.

It was a former Italian luxury liner seized by the U.S. and converted into a troop carrier.

It was huge, with probably six or seven decks altogether.

There were two- and five-level bunk beds everywhere, with narrow spaces in between so that we could move around.

They told us that there was an entire division on the ship. That's about 10,000 men. It sure was crowded.

It was February 1945, and the Atlantic was stormy the whole way over.

It was very choppy and almost everyone was sick, except for me and a few others.

So we did whatever we wanted to. The NCOs were sick, too, so they didn't make us work or anything.

There were 55-gallon drums everywhere, to throw up in. Most people weren't eating a thing, so we ended up eating very well.

The cooks weren't about to throw out all that good food, so they gave us the best stuff. We ate steak every single day!

It's worth taking a minute to describe how you eat under those conditions. Several rooms had been reserved for dining. The tables were wide and high, because you didn't sit down; you stood.

The tables were zinc-coated, with a lip about four inches high around the edge. Good thing, too!

Because, with the stormy weather, if you didn't hang on to your plate, it would slide to the other end of the table.

You couldn't put a cup down or even hold it full. You had to drink as soon as it was filled and then hold it in your hand or tie it to your belt.
Otherwise you'd lose it too.

Back in our sleeping quarters, the guy in the berth directly above mine must've weighed at least 300 pounds.

When he lay down (and that was often, because he was seasick and didn't move around much), I couldn't get into or out of my bunk, unless he got up.

He got up to be nice, but it made him mad because he felt really miserable.

His weight forced the bunk's canvas down and bent the support bars. When I was lying down, I could manage, I could even turn over if I made an effort, but I couldn't squeeze in between the two bars.

But I liked the idea of having the lower bunk, so I put up with it.

One day, in another part of the ship, I saw a guy in a two-level bunk bed who could actually sit up.

He had a deck of cards and was playing solitaire.

You're so lucky! I can't even sit on my own bed.

I told him why, and that's how I met Dominique d'Antona.

He was a quite masculine-looking Italian. He spoke in an educated and refined way and was very self-confident and ambitious.

We became friends and saw each other morning, noon, and night. We talked about music. He played the violin and had put together a quartet before he was drafted.

He always won at cards. He was generous and treated me to things.

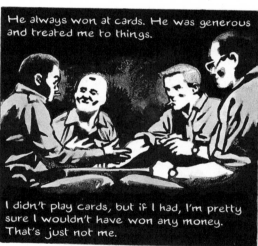

I didn't play cards, but if I had, I'm pretty sure I wouldn't have won any money. That's just not me.

Almost no one showered, because it was hard to do. The shower area had been designed to wash equipment, not people.

There was a pipe sticking out of the wall and absolutely nothing to hold onto. The wall and the floor were slippery and sticky.

It was a two-person job. One person would stand in a corner and the other would hose him down.

Funny how appalling the conditions were.

I loved the storm.

We weren't allowed to go outside, but we found an unlocked door that opened onto a small observation post that sat just above the waves.

We didn't tell anyone, and Dominique and I would go out to watch the storm.

In the morning, the waves were huge. When the ship was at the base of a wave, you could see the sunrise through the water.

The colors were amazing.

Military protocols continued throughout the crossing, so one day I was told:

Cope, you're promoted to first class.

Here are your stripes. You have something to sew them on with?

Yes.

Okay, sew them on right away.

That had taken a while! It got me a bit more money and made it easier for me to buy chocolate, Cokes, and cigarettes.

The army didn't pay us a lot.

Early one morning, we were suddenly informed: "We're disembarking!" Soon we were down on the dock.

We got our packs quickly; the distribution process ran smoothly. And when I say packs, I mean packs: we were loaded down with an incredible amount of stuff.

Usually you didn't have to carry everything; part of it would be loaded onto trucks. But there was no truck here. The sergeant said:

Pick up your things and follow me!

88

We were in France. As far as I know, in Le Havre. The city had been completely destroyed.

We saw what
the war had been like
before we got there.
At the time, of course,
the Germans were far away.

The road was in very bad shape.
The buildings on either side of us
had been reduced to rubble.

No one could carry this much stuff.
We tried to drag some of it behind us,
but that was forbidden.

The sergeant often
had us stop to rest.
It was during one
of those breaks
that Stanley, the guy
next to me, said:

Well, Cope!
We're not
about to
forget this
February 19th!

Today's February 19th?

Yup.

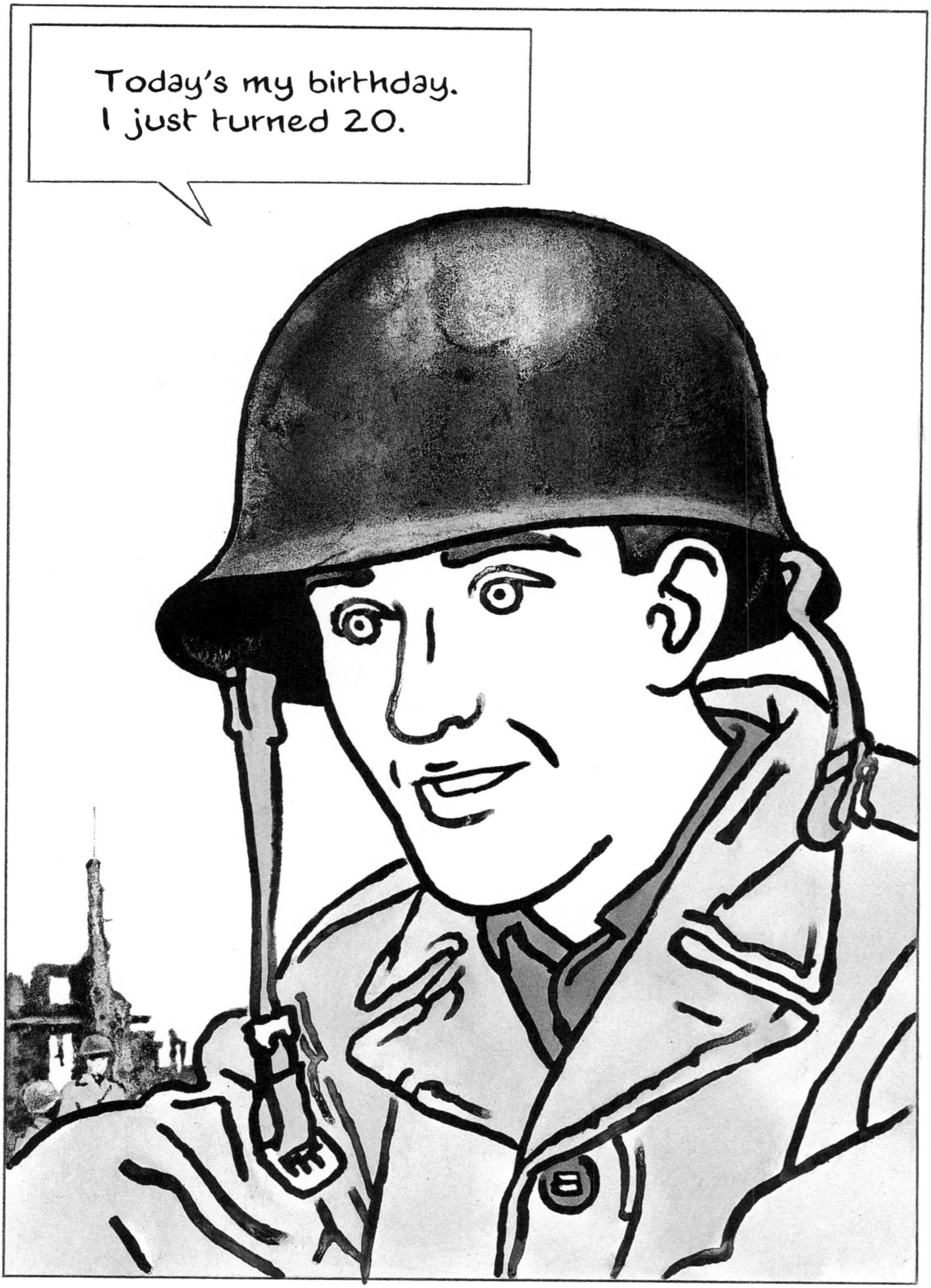
Today's my birthday.
I just turned 20.

14

I arrived in France on February 19, 1945, the day I turned 20.

They put us in "40 and 8" boxcars— very basic old wooden boxcars with sliding doors.

They were called "40 and 8" because their capacity was either 40 men or 8 horses, standing. They weren't meant to transport men lying down. And horses, as you know, don't lie down.

We waited for quite a while, and finally the train started to move, slowly, through a pretty dismal landscape.

Much destruction.

Sometimes we'd pass over a trench and we'd look down, out the door, but there was no track to be seen. All that remained were the rails—no crosspieces. They didn't give way, though.

The train stopped pretty often for a "piss call." Everyone got out and did what they had to do.

Night fell. The train passed between two high stone walls marked:

PARIS!

We're near Paris!

We're going to Paris!

Great!

The train stopped between those walls. We were forbidden to get out.

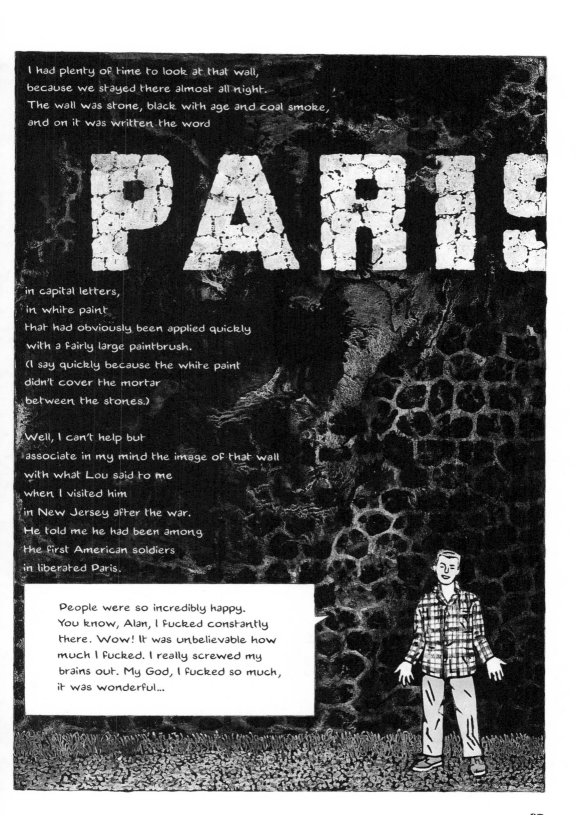

I had plenty of time to look at that wall,
because we stayed there almost all night.
The wall was stone, black with age and coal smoke,
and on it was written the word

PARIS

in capital letters,
in white paint
that had obviously been applied quickly
with a fairly large paintbrush.
(I say quickly because the white paint
didn't cover the mortar
between the stones.)

Well, I can't help but
associate in my mind the image of that wall
with what Lou said to me
when I visited him
in New Jersey after the war.
He told me he had been among
the first American soldiers
in liberated Paris.

People were so incredibly happy.
You know, Alan, I fucked constantly
there. Wow! It was unbelievable how
much I fucked. I really screwed my
brains out. My God, I fucked so much,
it was wonderful...

I, however, had been stuck in that train. We devised a system so that some of us could lie down. We'd take turns or just lie in a heap on top of one another.

The train started moving backward. All we ever saw of Paris was that dry riverbed, on the approach to a station—which one, I'll never know.

So all we had done was go to Paris to change tracks, and another locomotive took us back in the direction we'd come from.

Finally, the next day we ended up in Gournay-en-Bray, in Normandy.

15

We were stationed in Normandy for two months,
because the army had misplaced our weapons and our vehicles.

We were told: "Apparently no one knows where our vehicles are.
They didn't follow us like they were supposed to.
They went somewhere else."

All our armored cars, jeeps, cannons, machine guns, bazookas, and mortars
had been sent to the wrong place. We didn't have a single weapon.
Only the officers had guns. We didn't have a vehicle, either,
except for a few trucks that didn't even belong to us.

It was a completely crazy situation.

There I met up with Marker, Kulik, and Polski. We and the crew of another vehicle were housed behind a farm, on the first floor of a barn, along with two cows. Which was great, because cows give off a lot of heat.

There was very little farming going on there because there was hardly anyone left to do the work.

Next to our barn stood a small one-room house with a chimney but no windows, which the sergeants used as a command post. The captain stayed at another farm a bit farther away.

So we got two months' rest, more or less. It was a pretty boring life. We were taken on marches and had military manuals read to us, which we had to study. I spent my time chatting and wandering around.

Dominique d'Antona's unit was stationed on the other side of a small valley. I often went over to see him; he wasn't much of a hiker.

We had been told to be careful, that the enemy was everywhere, not to get too involved with the locals, etc.
That was mostly for training purposes, in preparation for the time when we'd really be in that kind of territory.

Of course, at the time, the Americans had barely made it across the Rhine. And there were still Germans in eastern France.
Lou, for instance, was caught in the terrible Battle of the Bulge, where a German counteroffensive surrounded the Allied forces.

I didn't pay too much attention to orders. Once it got dark, I'd set out through the woods to meet Dominique. I had a big knife my father had given me. It was a very long knife—a magnificent piece. I'd put it in my boot and cross the valley alone. I never ran into a soul.

I'd get to where Dominique was staying pretty quickly, and we'd go into Gournay together.

The place was a ghost town. You know, not all of France was damaged, but all of France had deteriorated. They didn't yet have anything to fix things with.

Dominique continued to win at card games and would often buy me a meal in a small café. The owner had figured out that he could make a fair amount of money by serving American soldiers.

There wasn't much to eat, but it was there that I had my first brandy.

It was also in that café that I saw, for the first time, toilets that consisted of a long wooden bench with two holes in it, side by side. Men and women used them, at the same time if need be.

Dominique had a dalliance going in Gournay, with a girl by the name of Mimi. She was very pretty. The thing was, he was already engaged to a girl back home, and he didn't want it to go too far. He'd say to me:

I've absolutely got to see Mimi, Alan, even though it gives me an awful pain in the balls.

So I'd go with him to her house, because alone he couldn't have resisted the temptation.

Dominique introduced me to one of his friends, Francis, who was a bit older than we were. We hit it off.
He really liked classical music.

Francis had met a young woman who had already made a name for herself as a budding concert pianist. Her name was Monique de La Brochellerie.

He took us to her house, which was just outside Gournay.

She was absolutely charming. She'd fled during the war and had only recently returned to her house and her piano.

Would you be kind enough to play something for Alan?

Sure, but you know, since I haven't played in such a long time, I haven't really gotten my fingers back.

She started playing Beethoven sonatas. Sure enough, she sometimes made mistakes and had to start over, but it was clear that she played very, very well.

Four years later, in Paris, I saw in the paper that Monique de La Brochellerie was giving a concert.

103

Naturally, I went to the concert. She played the "Moonlight Sonata," just as she had four years earlier, but wonderfully, with no hesitation.

Most of the program was made up of pieces by Scarlatti, which I love. I've since tried to play a bit of his work myself.

Afterward I went to see her in her dressing room. I introduced myself. She was delighted to see me again.

Do you know what happened to Francis? He wrote to me for a while and all of sudden I stopped hearing from him.

Same here. I tried to reach him, but without success.

He had a delicate constitution. I had often wondered if he'd gotten sick.

In fact, although we didn't want to say it, we were both thinking that he might have been killed in combat. He had been very fond of her.

So there you have it. I had found Monique de La Brochellerie once again. I almost always meet up again with the people I care about, in the most unexpected circumstances.

There's not much to say about Gournay. Or, yes, wait a minute—I did have a frightening experience in the barn.

As I mentioned earlier, we were living right over the cows.

It was very high up. You used a metal ladder hooked to a bar to reach the little door leading to the roof.

Everyone else went up and down in the usual way, facing the ladder, except me. I was pretty agile, so I'd descend by catching the rungs with my heels and sliding down with my back against the ladder.

Cope! What are you doing? It's dangerous!

No it isn't. I'm managing pretty well, don't you think? I can even do it carrying stuff.

One day I was on my way to do laundry, which I usually did by building a fire, heating some water, and washing my things in my helmet. So I went out that little door, like I always did, without looking, my dirty laundry in one hand and my helmet in the other.

Someone had moved the ladder.

I plummeted to the ground.

It was a rough landing. I hurt my ankles quite badly, and my hands and arms were bleeding.

After the war, they awarded Purple Hearts to every soldier who'd been hurt. The sergeant asked me:

Cope, were you ever wounded?

No.

Not even a scratch, or a cut, or anything?

Oh, yes!

I told him the story of the ladder. He said: "Oh! Well, that's worth a Purple Heart!" Haha! That's how I got my medal.

Before telling you about our departure from Gournay, why don't I describe Marker, Kulik, and Polski? Quickly:

A lot of the guys called Marker "John," or just "Marker." Even though I was probably the serviceman closest to him, I always called him "Sergeant Marker." As a sign of respect, I suppose.
He knew he could always count on me, and I think he appreciated my courtesy.
He was a really great guy.
He was maybe 25 years old.
After the war, we wrote to each other for a while—I even corresponded with his sister—but we eventually lost touch.

We called our driver by his last name, which was, I'm almost certain, Polski. I remember that when Marker called him and he didn't move fast enough, he'd yell out: "Hey, Polack!"
And when Polski arrived, every time he'd tell him, "Marker, my name is Polski!"
His parents were, of course, Polish, and he spoke Polish. He was the one who in civilian life drove trucks loaded with dynamite. He was 23 at the time.
He was small and thin but muscular, with blue eyes and dishwater blond hair.
He was nice, but not very smart.
You could see he'd had a hard life.
He looked kind of worn.

Kulik, the radio operator, was a New York Jew, 22 or 23 years old.
He was fairly tall, kind of pudgy.
He had short, straight black hair.
He shaved regularly but always had a five o'clock shadow. His hands were plump and hairy. He was very nice.
His parents owned a deli in New York, and sent him care package after care package. Thanks to them and him, we ate like kings.

Above Marker there was a staff sergeant in charge of three armored vehicles, including ours. His name was Kubacek.
He was tall, not really athletic, but burly.
He had light brown hair, large eyes, and always wore an annoyed, sour look on his face.
We weren't too fond of him.

That's it for the group portrait.

Finally, our vehicles arrived.
A great commotion ensued, because they had to be cleaned.

Each piece of metal equipment had been coated with a thick, hard layer of Cosmoline grease. It did a great job of protecting things during transport, but it was a real pain to remove.

You got rid of it with gasoline, which eventually did the job after plenty of scrubbing. So some people were assigned to de-Cosmoline the weapons.

I had to do it only once, thank God— it was one of the worst chores.

The .50 caliber machine gun, the big machine gun with handles that was going to be mounted on our armored car, was de-Cosmolined by a guy named Kraus, a corporal I didn't like one bit.

He took advantage of everyone.

That day there was a fire in the little house next to our barn. Kraus was on duty. It was quite a fire. He gave some explanation; I don't remember what it was. He was a liar anyway.

So we left at last. Our two-month interlude was over.
We'd been living an incredible life, sitting on our hands like that.

Still, everyone was pretty happy to see it come to an end.

We were setting out on an amazing journey.

16

It might have been April 8, or even April 15.
Everything was gray and dirty. It was freezing cold,
but it was springtime nonetheless.

We drove only on country roads,
not major highways.
I really enjoyed watching the scenery go by from high up in my turret.

It was like something out of a children's
history book—quaint.

For an American like me, though, everything there was quaint.

I was discovering Europe's little villages.
We don't have villages like that where I come from.
They were charming—tree-lined streets, fields, farms,
the things we saw through the windows—
everything was different and fascinated me, you know?

I hadn't expected my war to be like that.
Some people pay a fortune to see a foreign country,
but here I was, seeing it from my turret.
Even though it was wartime, every day was a real journey.

Some of last fall's apples still hung on the apple trees that lined the roads. It was fun to grab one as we drove under their branches.

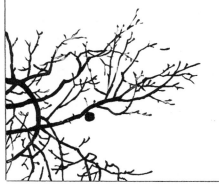

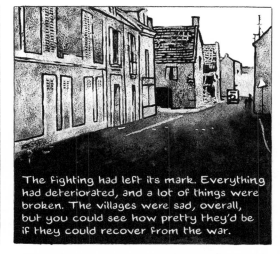

The fighting had left its mark. Everything had deteriorated, and a lot of things were broken. The villages were sad, overall, but you could see how pretty they'd be if they could recover from the war.

Polski, because of his civilian job, was a kind of daredevil who had no fear when it came to driving. He came up with a game.

He'd let our vehicle trail behind the column, which was very short because we traveled in platoons, with a lot of space in between them so that we wouldn't all be wiped out at once if we were attacked.

Our platoon consisted of three armored cars. We drove in second place, which forced the third car to slow down as well, infuriating its driver.

Polski let our car fall very far behind, and right before we reached a village, he suddenly hit the gas.

Those armored cars could go 80 miles an hour. And they were massive.

We entered the village at top speed.

It was one of those old towns with no sidewalks, whose streets hadn't yet been straightened out. There were sharp turns.

His game involved grazing the walls, first on one side and then on the other, hitting them just hard enough to scrape off some of the plaster.

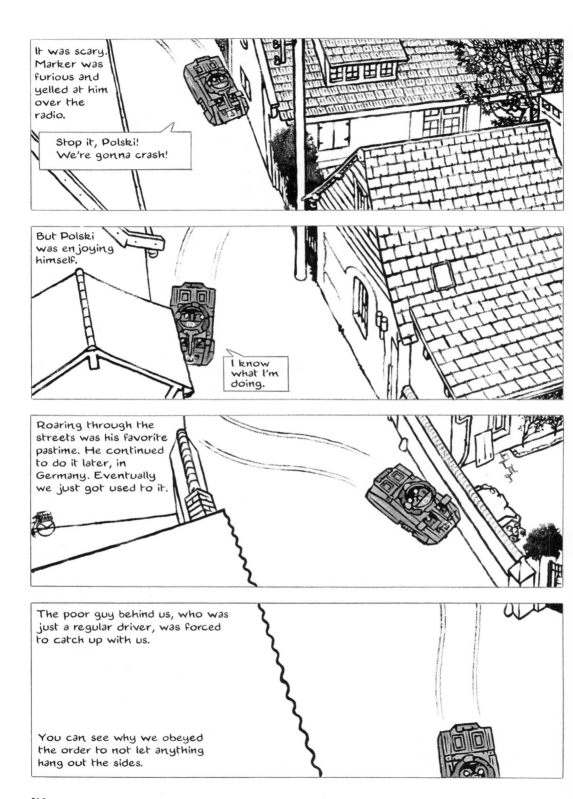

It was scary. Marker was furious and yelled at him over the radio.

Stop it, Polski! We're gonna crash!

But Polski was enjoying himself.

I know what I'm doing.

Roaring through the streets was his favorite pastime. He continued to do it later, in Germany. Eventually we just got used to it.

The poor guy behind us, who was just a regular driver, was forced to catch up with us.

You can see why we obeyed the order to not let anything hang out the sides.

On the first night of the trip, as we did most other nights after that, we bivouacked.
A bit about bivouacking...
Last century, apparently, at West Point, future officers were partly instructed in French.
As a matter of fact, Anglo-Saxon military terminology comes almost entirely from the French and Latin.
Ranks, for instance—general, captain, lieutenant, sergeant—they're all the same in French.
As young soldiers from a country where there was no military service and there hadn't been a draft since World War I, we were completely ignorant of that vocabulary.
The first time I heard "We're going to bivouac tonight" was during military training.
I said to myself, "My God, what are we going to be doing?"
They sounded reveille in the mornings.
Nearly everybody knew what that was because it was used in the Boy Scouts.
But we didn't know that "reveille" means "awakening" in French.
When I became a soldier, I also learned the meaning of the word "latrines," which comes from Latin.
In civilian life, we never call toilets latrines, do we?
There were all kinds of words like that.

Anyway, the first night we bivouacked somewhere in France. Where, I have no idea. There was certainly no danger of any Germans showing up, but someone had to stand guard nonetheless.

Cope, you're standing guard. It's just for show, but we've gotta do it. It's totally idiotic.

Okay.

Anyway, you'll stand over there, next to that trench, and, if you want to, a little later, when everyone's gone to bed, you can lie down too, in the trench.

I'd rather have you get some sleep than follow that completely stupid rule.

Plus, there were a lot of other units all around us.

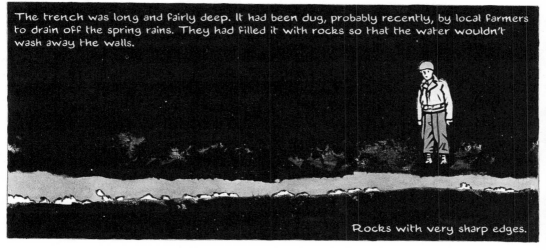

The trench was long and fairly deep. It had been dug, probably recently, by local farmers to drain off the spring rains. They had filled it with rocks so that the water wouldn't wash away the walls.

Rocks with very sharp edges.

Well, believe it or not, I spent a great night there. First of all, I was exhausted. And then I figured out that if you were careful, you could bend yourself in among all those different shapes. I slept like a baby—to my great surprise.

Soon we arrived at a place where there was a flurry of people and vehicles.

Left and right, units were on the move. We passed soldiers returning from the front; you could tell they'd seen combat. The roads were crowded, but we managed to keep going.

The next night, we requisitioned a small farm to sleep in. The French farmer was staying in another building. We were getting ready to lie down on the floor in our sleeping bags in what looked like a dining room, with a fireplace.

We asked the farmer for some wood.

Pas de bois.

We were disappointed because we'd been on the road all day, it was raining, and we were cold.

So one of our guys pointed to his garden fence, made of wooden posts wired together.

He didn't understand English, but he understood what the soldier meant.

Non. Pas ma clôture.

In the corner of the room stood a wooden table and two chairs. The soldier went over to the table and started to break off one of its legs.

When the farmer saw that, he ran outside and pulled his fence posts out himself. We had wire cutters, so we were able to build a fire.

It really wasn't a very nice thing to do, but that's how it was. I wasn't part of the operation, but I have to say that I did warm myself in front of the fire.

We were nearing the Rhine, and one thing had us worried: our turret was missing its rail. That meant we couldn't set up our machine gun, which is the only truly effective weapon for that kind of vehicle.

Marker had grown anxious.

Can you believe that these idiots are sending us into combat with just our rifles and this useless cannon?

The following night, our unit's NCOs got together.

Okay, guys, we have to find a rail for Kubacek's platoon. Let's do some midnight requisitioning.

Midnight requisitioning is exactly what it sounds like. You go out at midnight and requisition whatever you want.

Meaning, you just steal it.

So they came back with a rail, saying they took it off a vehicle that wasn't headed for the front.

They installed the rail on the turret and set up the machine gun on it, which made all of us feel better.

The next day, after another endless drive, we reached the Rhine.

17

On the other side was Germany.

We had to cross a floating bridge. It looked awfully narrow.

Barely wide enough for an armored car like ours.

In the end, we got across fine.

I think we were probably around Bade-Würtemberg. I must say that at the time, I knew nothing about geography. I was an ignoramus.

Believe it or not, all the way from the Rhine to Pilsen, in Czechoslovakia, we didn't go through a single big city. We really weren't taking the main roads. I loved the scenery. We tried to make out the names of the villages if they were marked—everything seemed to end in "hausen" or something like it.

During one of our first bivouacs in Germany, something terrible happened to me. You know that during military bivouacs, you have to dig a hole to shit in and then cover it up with dirt.

I was assigned the job. I dug the hole and then I used it.

While I was crouched over, I got stung on the penis by a mosquito.

The swelling was terrible, it hurt, and it got really enormous. I couldn't do anything but wait for it to go away.

It took two days. It hurt like hell to walk because it was getting mashed between my legs.

It's probably better if you don't draw that.

Let me tell you about the only time I used the machine gun during the war. We were way out in the countryside, and suddenly we heard gunfire.

We didn't know if we were the targets. Shots rang out nearby, but the loudest ones came from far away.

We could see a farm with people running around in all directions as if they were about to do something, but they weren't shooting.
So we didn't fire at them.

A bit farther, in the middle of a field, sat a tiny little house. Sergeant Marker said:

Cope, that building's dangerous, the perfect place to hide weapons. We shouldn't leave it standing.

What should we do?

123

You're going to fire the cannon. Let's come to a full stop so you can shoot while we're not in motion.

So we maneuvered into position, he gave the order, I aimed and...

BOOM.
I got it.

The house basically collapsed. I don't know what there'd been inside. No people, in any case. They were over at the farm.

TA

We were happy to see that the cannon worked properly and that I was still a good shot. That's probably what Marker wanted to check, anyway.

Later, we came under fire for real, from a farm on a hill.

TA   TA

Okay, fire again.

This time we were going to use the machine gun, not the cannon.

I fired. We had tracer ammunition rounds—you know what they are? One out of every five or ten rounds leaves a small light trail, so you can see its path. Otherwise, you have no idea where your machine gun fire is going.

TA TA TA   TA

I was firing into the farm's courtyard. We heard shooting from up there, but no more bullets came our way.

TATA TA TA TA T

TA

All of a sudden my machine gun jammed.

What's going on, Cope?

No clue!

It was unbelievable. I regularly took it apart to clean and oil, before carefully putting it back together. I truly took good care of it.

We found a sheltered spot. We took the gun apart and saw that the bolt had split in two. The bolt is the part of the gun that goes back and forth, pushing bullets into the firing chamber and expelling the spent shell casings.

Split in two! We'd never heard of such a thing!

The machine gun was completely out of commission—
Marker was furious. We got back on the road.
Luckily, I didn't need to shoot again in the days that followed,
because we weren't able to get another bolt until much later.
By the time we no longer needed it, in fact.

Marker suspected something.
A short while later, he went to find Kraus,
the corporal who had de-Cosmolined
our weapon.

Kraus finally admitted what had happened.
Remember, he'd been on duty the day
the sergeants' little command post burned
down, back in Normandy.

As there was nothing to do that day, no
messages to be received, nothing to do
but sit quietly in a nice warm place,
he'd been given weapons-cleaning duty.

Kraus was de-Cosmolining our machine
gun bolt in a fuel drum that he had put
near the fireplace so he could stay warm.
Too near, as it turns out.

The house caught fire, and the poor bolt sat there God knows how long inside a burning fuel drum.

Kraus never said a word when we went to pick it up. The fire had crystallized the steel, which shattered the first time it was used.

I should have you court-martialed.

We got out of it okay, so I won't turn you in this time. But watch out— I'm keeping an eye on you.

Kraus could be sweet and kind, but it was pure hypocrisy. You've met the type, haven't you?

The army had all kinds of people.

Shortly thereafter, we arrived at a village, which, based on what I later learned about Germany, I'm pretty sure was in northern Swabia.

The townspeople lined the streets, greeting us with enthusiasm. But their happiness probably owed more to the thought that the war would soon be over than to seeing Americans.

On a little street corner, right in front of a house, under some nice trees, a family was offering to sell two cases of white wine to passing vehicles.

The troops ahead of us were suspicious and turned them down.

Should we take them?

Yeah.

What if they're poisoned?

We'll figure a way to find out. But I'd be really surprised if they were.

We took everything. We never had received any ammunition for the cannon—five or six shells, tops. So we put the wine bottles in the empty ammunition compartments. They just fit.

That's how we got that supply of wine. It was a delicious Baden wine. And so I continued the wine apprenticeship I had begun in Normandy.

Back in California, I had drunk maybe a glass or two at the most—nothing very good.

Maybe it's time to talk about what we ate.
First of all, we had rations. K rations.
They came in a small container shaped like
a videotape case but about twice the size.
Each one held a single meal.
We had a whole bunch of them—
they were everywhere.
They were wrapped in very thick,
waterproof paper, and they could sit in water
for days without the food getting wet.

The meals were very cleverly arranged.
There was corned beef, not as good as French pâté,
but meat nonetheless.
There were biscuits, like hardtack, instead of bread,
not very tasty but nutritious; dessert—a kind of
pudding; and there was always a chocolate bar.

Then there was a small amount of powdered
coffee with a bit of sugar, which you could
have hot or cold if you had water, and a small
package of powdered fruit juice that was
supposed to taste like grape;
we called it "bug juice."
I've never eaten a bug, but I imagine that's
probably what it would taste like.

Plus there were packs of three cigarettes,
not brand-name cigarettes, but we were glad
to have them. They were well wrapped
and came with matches.

The army had figured out how to fit as much
as possible into a small space.

I never turned up my nose at field rations. A lot of soldiers didn't like them, but I always enjoyed eating them. I had a hearty appetite.

But it goes without saying that army-issue food couldn't compare with Kulik's care packages. I mentioned earlier that his parents owned a deli in New York. I don't know if all their packages arrived, but in any case we got a lot of them, and they were full of absolutely delicious stuff.

There were quite a few delicious Jewish specialty dishes: smoked sausage, top-quality wursts. There was so much of it we had trouble finding a place to put everything, so we'd hide things under canvas tarps tied to the side of the car. In theory, we weren't supposed to tie anything there, but almost everyone did anyway.

Polski, needless to say, stopped slaloming through villages.

We'd stop to eat, usually by the side of the road, leaving some distance between vehicles. We ate together, trying to keep out of sight. We chowed down the food and drank that delicious wine, which we rationed so it would last longer—one glass with each meal.

We would have liked to be more generous with the other cars, but we thought to ourselves, "The day'll come when we might not have anything left to eat. As long as we can find a place to put the stuff, we'll keep it."

In all that time, I received next to nothing.
Oh, I didn't care.
After all, everything I'm telling you about took place in the space of just a few months. Plus, at the tail end of hostilities, it's possible that the postal service didn't even know where we were, because our military mission was pretty bizarre.
I'll explain.

18

We had huge amounts of gasoline. We were forbidden to wash our clothes in it, which made sense, but we did anyway.

We'd hang our fatigues from the back of the car so they wouldn't smell too strongly of gas. The wind would dry them quickly and the odor would dissipate.

So we were always clean, and we liked it that way. Of course, we did a lot of things we weren't supposed to, but I think that nonetheless we were good soldiers.

We drove long distances. Sometimes we'd sleep only every second or third night. Exhaustion and lack of sleep began affecting us more and more, not to mention stress and sometimes outright fear.
We'd already seen disturbing sights, including corpses.

One evening, as night was falling—I couldn't tell you where we were—we stopped in a residential sort of neighborhood, where there were some fairly nice houses.

The houses had been requisitioned, and people—mostly women and children, of course—were coming out of them carrying pillows, blankets, comforters, and clothes.

They were going to spend the night a bit farther up the road, with neighbors or friends, leaving us their empty homes.

Because we didn't requisition too many houses, the rooms were packed.
We were now going to be able to get a few hours' sleep. We were supposed to get up at dawn.

I remember that the house we went into was already occupied by the crews of another armored car and two Jeeps. There were a lot of us.

The cellar had been converted into a living space. There were two rooms, with a big bed in each. Kubacek said:

You, in there.

There was Stanley, a guy named Louis, and me.

Louis was with one of the company's four Jeeps. He was a bit of a bastard, but I liked him. I teamed up with him to go on patrol. He was the rugged type, real tall and strong, but completely uneducated and a bit crazy.

We had eaten and smoked a cigarette, and all we wanted to do was sleep. But Louis had found something to drink. By the time we went to bed, he was dead drunk.

I was in the middle and Stanley against the wall. Once we got settled and were almost asleep, Louis started to say things I understood the meaning of quite well.

He grabbed me and started doing the things you do when you want to make love to someone.

I was furious, I shoved him, I yelled at him, but he kept saying:

Come on! You're cute!

By that time Stanley was beside himself. Instead of just giving him a shove, as I had, he went on the offensive. Louis gave up and fell asleep right away.

The next day he didn't look embarrassed at all. I didn't mention what had happened, and he didn't seem to remember a thing. His attitude remained exactly the same as before.

There was something strange about our journey now. It seemed to me that we'd wandered far from where we were supposed to be. The officers had orders to press forward, but they had no maps. We kept going.

There were a lot of accidents, especially at night. Many roads and bridges had been destroyed, and in wartime you don't use your headlights. Some guys died because all of a sudden, in the dark, they'd find themselves at the end of a road and SPLASH, they'd fall in.

Something like that happened to us on a tiny country road, probably somewhere in Bavaria. It was a moonless night. We were driving with blackened lights, meaning we'd covered our headlights with hoods slit down the middle. We couldn't make out a thing, but we could be seen by the other vehicles from a distance of perhaps ten feet.

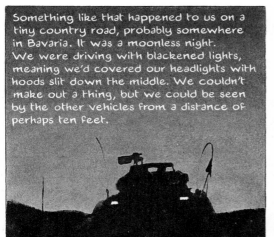

We'd driven for two days and two nights without stopping. Polski was exhausted.

My eyes are closing—I can't drive anymore. What do we do?

Marker said to me:

Cope, take his place.

Kulik was afraid of driving the armored car. He was awful at it.

I wasn't used to driving, especially under those conditions, but I managed. The road was full of sharp turns. I followed the Jeep ahead of me.

All of a sudden, the Jeep was gone.

I said to myself: "Don't just think you're imagining things. Stop."

I spoke into the microphone:

I'm stopping because the Jeep disappeared.

What do you mean, the Jeep disappeared?

The road had crumbled, right where there was a particularly sharp turn. So instead of making the turn, the Jeep had fallen straight into a giant pit.

It had landed nose down. No one was hurt, but they were climbing back up the hill, terrified we'd be right behind them and run them over.

That's what would have happened if I hadn't had the brains to stop.

Armored cars have winches, so that's how we pulled them back up. The Jeep was fine, and we got back on the road.

We drove all the next day. It was becoming surreal. We kept wondering where we were going, and why we were in such a hurry.

By nightfall, we had arrived at a place where they made us get out of our vehicles, but not to sleep.

We're going on patrol.

They explained to us our patrol plan, and teams were formed. I was with Louis once again. Leaving our vehicles well guarded, we took off.

Louis was ahead of me. He was carrying the small machine gun, and I had the tripod. Because you had to be flat on your stomach half the time, one person couldn't carry both.

In an emergency, he could have used the machine gun without the tripod, although it was pretty heavy. When we had the time, I'd set up the tripod and we'd mount the gun on it.

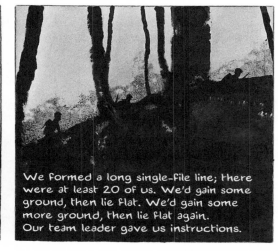

We formed a long single-file line; there were at least 20 of us. We'd gain some ground, then lie flat. We'd gain some more ground, then lie flat again.
Our team leader gave us instructions.

Louis was so tired that each time he lay down, he'd fall asleep immediately. I could even hear him snoring.

When it was time to go, I'd hit his feet hard with the tripod to wake him.

Then I hallucinated—for the first and only time in my life.

On my right there lay a long, steep rise of the kind that's typical in areas of rolling hills. I was looking at it.

German bombs, or maybe it was mortar fire, fell in the distance, intermittingly illuminating the sky. They didn't reach us, though.

All of a sudden, a gigantic city—huge buildings with brightly lit windows— appeared on the hill.

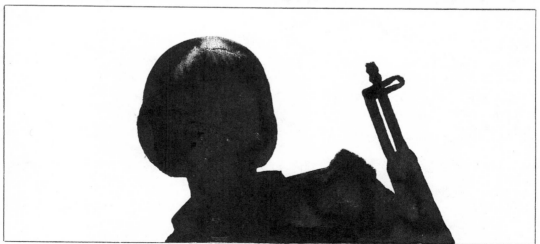

You had to see it to believe it.

I knew I was gazing at something that wasn't there. I really saw all those lights, as if they shined from all sorts of buildings. It was marvelous.

And then we had to move on again.
I forced myself to not see the city, and it disappeared.

We checked out a bunch of houses in an old village where Germans were supposed to be hiding.

It was pretty spooky, ghostly even. We were entering houses we didn't know, and we had to do it in the dark. There was no one there, only crushed cigarette butts and empty bottles.

Coming back down through the woods, on the edge of a clearing, we saw a German patrol pass by.

We were four, including Marker. He said to me:

I don't see any reason to do anything.

Me neither.

We'll have to wait for daylight. Let's dig a trench.

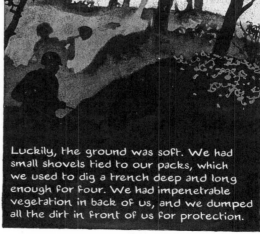

Luckily, the ground was soft. We had small shovels tied to our packs, which we used to dig a trench deep and long enough for four. We had impenetrable vegetation in back of us, and we dumped all the dirt in front of us for protection.

You'd better believe we didn't smoke or use our flashlights and spoke only in whispers. Actually, we hardly spoke to each other at all. We were determined to make as little noise as possible and just wait.

It was an endless night. We did what we could to try to make out things in the dark, to see what was on the other side of the clearing.

Several times Marker said to me:

Do you see someone moving over there?

Could be.

I think it was just our imagination.

Finally, dawn.
There was no one.

We returned to the place where we had left the vehicles. Everyone explained what they had seen and done. And then we got back on the road, utterly exhausted.

19

Finally, we came to some two-bit town where there was a hotel. We were ordered to stop, walk to the hotel, pick a room, and go to sleep.

We ate some rations, collapsed onto our beds, and, as you can imagine, slept soundly.

At around 4 a.m., a dispatch rider went door to door:

Everybody up and out! Go to your vehicles.

He forgot to open our door.

Once everyone was downstairs and ready, Kubacek noticed our empty armored car.

Where are Marker and his men?

They went back upstairs to get us. For once we'd indulged in the luxury of sleeping in only our shorts, so we had to run out of there, dragging behind us our gear and our clothes, and get dressed in the vehicle.

We were still heading east, but at that point we really had no maps at all.

As we drove slowly through a small village, the armored car ahead of us suddenly leapt into the air. It had hit a mine.

It wasn't damaged, but it bounced so hard that the driver hit his head and was groggy for a few days, with headaches and dizziness...

That made us mad, and we decided that, for revenge, we would loot the place. My buddies and I said, "We've never looted, everyone loots, we have to loot."

We went into a house, and I took a watch from a dresser drawer. The others also took watches, rings, that kind of stuff.

A few months later, when I was with the occupation forces in southern Germany, we drew lots to buy a watch, and I won.

145

I was friends with a young serviceman named Kinney, who wanted to be a pastor. He didn't have a watch. I bought one and gave him the one I'd taken. He was thrilled.

Two days later, I explained how I'd gotten it. He didn't want to wear it anymore, but I persuade him to keep it on.

Come on, why not? Wear the watch. You're my friend. Wear it.

So he wore it. There's another little story.

That was the only time I did any looting during the war.
We were all nice kids without much experience. Most of us had to force ourselves to go into houses and loot. Some guys thought it was fun, others didn't.
But sometimes we'd run into soldiers from other units who'd been more involved in the war and who often talked about looting.
It happened a lot.
There'd be small thefts from people to get this or that thing you wanted.

That same day, Stanley, a friend I mentioned earlier, a Jeep rifleman, was sent on a recon mission. His Jeep left along with three or four others. It was a potentially dangerous mission.

They returned that night, and he said to me:

We saw something horrible.

We were driving on a road bordering a sort of quarry. Inside, there were soldiers from a German patrol. They were all leaning against the quarry walls, standing up, with their mouths open, dead.

It was creepy seeing them dead, but still upright. They must have been relatively high-ranking, because they all had nice guns in their holsters—Lügers.

Here, I brought you one, Alan. With its holster.

I said to myself, "Well, I've got a souvenir." I was happy to have it.

A year later, when I returned to the States as a civilian, customs officials tried to take it from me when I disembarked in New York.

The same thing happened to quite a few people with me. Everyone was so disappointed that we threw our weapons into the water rather than give them to customs.

As we drove on, we saw the scenery change. In fact, without knowing it, we were leaving Germany and entering Czechoslovakia.

Suddenly, we heard an incredible barrage of noises up ahead—tanks firing. We were soon driving past houses burning to the ground.

It was the city of Pilsen.
Our tanks were taking it from the Germans.

The Jeeps and three armored cars stopped in a square. Crowds of Czechs shouted to us "SLAVA! SLAVA!" It can mean whatever you want it to— hello, good-bye, congratulations— but, in any case, it's a good thing.

So then Kubacek, our staff sergeant, climbed onto his armored car, raised his arms in the air, got the crowd to quiet down somewhat, and launched into a big speech in Czech.

He had a Central or Eastern European name, but there are so many different nationalities in the States, we young and ignorant Americans had never wondered where he was from. We were stunned.

The crowd was responding to him—it was an amazing moment. We all were laughing, saying to each other, "It's unbelievable, Kubacek is giving them a speech in their own language!"

And then snipers started shooting at us.

The crowd scattered, and we were ordered to go into the buildings and hunt them down.

So that's what we did. I heard a few nearby, but I didn't see any. There weren't many of them, and they were eliminated pretty quickly.

In fact, all the Germans in Pilsen quickly surrendered.

I think now's the time to describe our special mission, and say why we were there.

General Patton was the one who'd decided we'd be going to Pilsen.
He'd wanted us to go even farther.
The idea was to take as much ground as possible from the Russians.
That's why we'd been driving so fast for days and days without stopping.
Eisenhower himself probably didn't know we'd go so far east,
because he never agreed to it.
We were a forward scouting party, and there weren't many of us.
The bulk of the troops was at least two hours behind us.
Two hours is a lot.
The tank company ahead of us, the one that took the city, was quite small.
When the German officers found that out, they told our officers:
"If we'd known you were just a reconnaissance unit, we would have annihilated you."
But our tanks, on Patton's orders, made so much noise coming into town
that the Germans believed an entire army had arrived.
It worked.

I'm pretty sure that that night we slept in our vehicles, parked in the street.

The next day I was promoted to corporal. It was great; it meant higher pay. I sewed on my stripes.

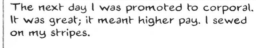

A bit later we were told to put on our Sunday best and show up clean-shaven, shoes shined and vehicles spick-and-span, because we were going on a mission and had to look good.

Our company— three armored cars and four Jeeps—drove to a small airport just outside Pilsen, in the middle of the woods.

Go chop down some big branches from the forest, to put some flagpoles up on your vehicles.

Which we did. Ours was secured to the turret.

Then they handed out beautiful, brand-new white nylon parachutes.

Cut them up so that each vehicle has a white flag, and tie it securely to the flagpole.

Each one of you should also cut out a large square, fold it diagonally, and tie it around your neck, like a long scarf, so that it hangs nicely behind your back.

We wondered what on earth this was all about.

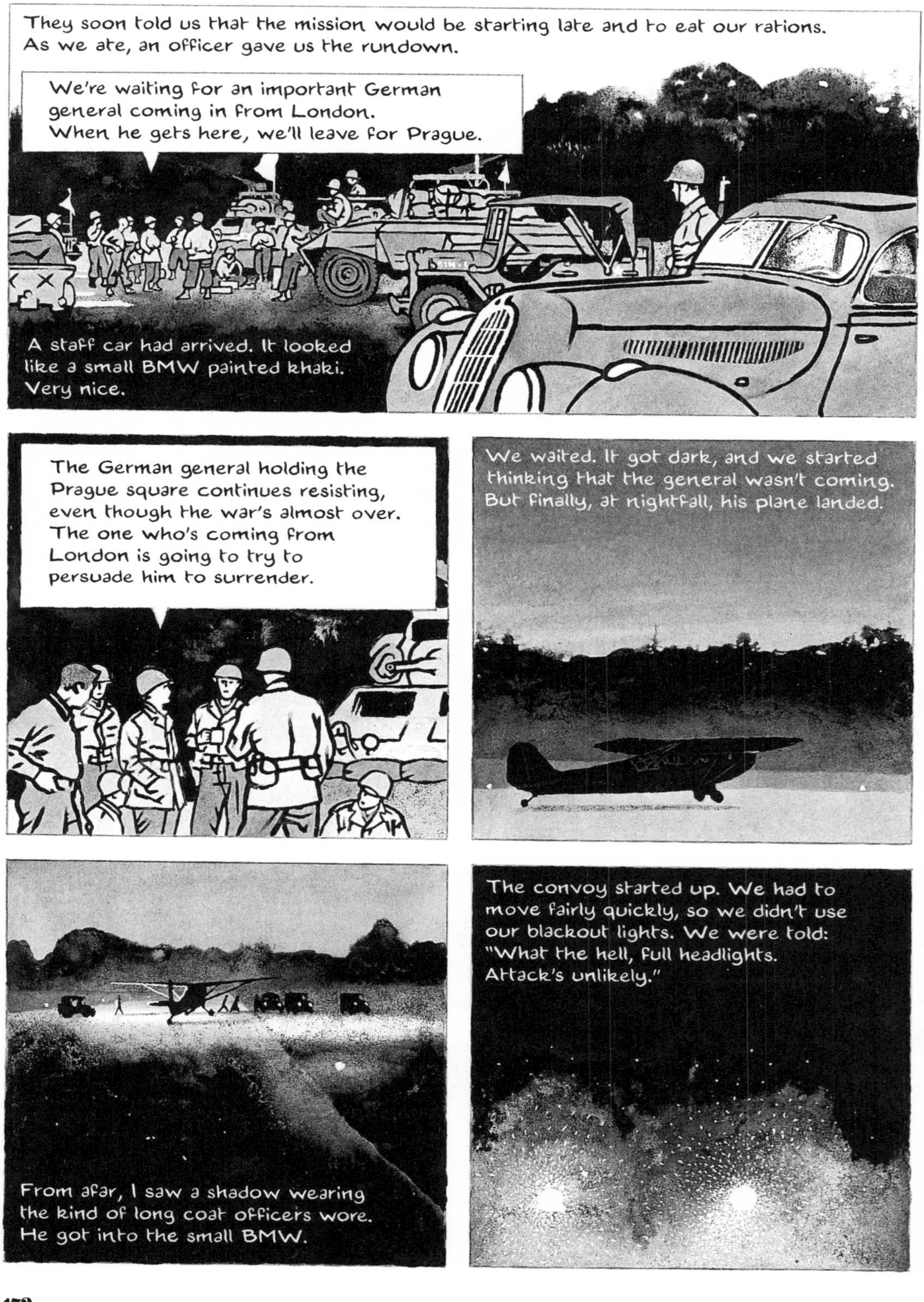
They soon told us that the mission would be starting late and to eat our rations. As we ate, an officer gave us the rundown.
We're waiting for an important German general coming in from London. When he gets here, we'll leave for Prague.
A staff car had arrived. It looked like a small BMW painted khaki. Very nice.
The German general holding the Prague square continues resisting, even though the war's almost over. The one who's coming from London is going to try to persuade him to surrender.
We waited. It got dark, and we started thinking that the general wasn't coming. But finally, at nightfall, his plane landed.
From afar, I saw a shadow wearing the kind of long coat officers wore. He got into the small BMW.
The convoy started up. We had to move fairly quickly, so we didn't use our blackout lights. We were told: "What the hell, full headlights. Attack's unlikely."

20

We reached Prague at midnight.

There were barricades at the entrance to the city—there'd been an uprising.

We asked them to take down their barricades so that we could get through, and they did. The barricades were mostly cobblestones torn up from the streets.

We drove toward the city center. There weren't any electric lights. Wood fires, not too far apart, replaced lampposts on the main avenues.

I glimpsed the silhouette of a cathedral.

Our officers and the German went inside the Prague German headquarters. There they were told that the person in charge had left and was now in a barracks just outside the city, to the east.

New, strict orders were given: no bullets in our weapon chambers, don't return fire if shot at, unless ordered to by an officer. If we did, we'd be court-martialed. We were supposed to just take the bullets, hoping we didn't die.

We turned east onto a long, wide avenue.

In the opposite direction, coming toward us, a column of German tanks appeared.

They were huge machines, very slow.

As is customary in urban areas in noncombat situations, a soldier walked ahead of each tank to guide the driver.

I thought, "What's going to happen here?"

Nothing happened. We started to pass them.

The German soldiers guiding the tanks looked flabbergasted to see us like that, Americans with white flags and white scarves, as if surrendering.

There were a lot of them. Their tanks moved slowly and so did we. As we reached one of the tanks, the short German soldier walking ahead of it looked at us with such amazement that he stopped cold, his mouth open, like a kid.

I realized his driver couldn't see that he'd stopped, that he was going to hit him.

So I gesticulated wildly, trying to let them know. Marker, who was on my right and couldn't see anything because of his angle, grabbed me.

What's your problem, Cope? You can't wave to the Germans!

I shouted: **Look!**

The little German soldier was pulled under by the tread.

The poor guy was crushed slowly, from his feet all the way to his head—with enough time to scream and thrash around wildly.

I think the driver never noticed. He probably thought that the guy had left his post, because the tank continued on as if nothing had happened.

There was absolutely nothing left of the little soldier. Even his helmet was squashed flat.

Pretty horrendous, to say the least.

We reached the barracks outside the city.

Our officers went inside and came out again, saying that the general had gone even farther east, to a village near the Polish border.

We got back on the road and stopped twice at town halls, where gasoline was secretly kept in the basement.

We filled the tank and stocked up on fuel. It was a terrible kind of gasoline that made our vehicles spew trails of black smoke. But it did make them move.

When we got back, we had to scrub out the carburetors.

By morning we were fairly close to our destination. Czech partisans fired shots at us from the woods.

In their place, I might have done the same.

They had no reason to think we were Americans; they probably thought it was some sort of German trick.

Later on, we passed long lines of German soldiers on foot. Most of them were wounded, some of them even pushed along in wheelbarrows by their buddies. They looked pathetic.

We swore at them. They didn't even answer. Maybe it wasn't a nice thing to do, but we did it anyway.

Finally, we got to the village. There was a small barracks that was set up kind of like a cavalry unit, with horse stalls. It was an elegant white building.

We were ushered into a dining hall, with the exact number of places set for us.

Each place setting had a knife, a small plate, a tiny slice of bread, a pat of butter, and a very thin slice of salami. And a cup.

Two or three German soldiers arrived and poured some bad ersatz coffee, without any sugar, into the cups. It was the German general who'd wanted to receive us like this.

It seemed clear to us that the general had been trying to draw us as far east as possible so that the Russians wouldn't enter Czechoslovakia. He had hoped that we'd be followed by the whole American army. That was certainly Patton's idea as well.

I don't know if there's any record of our mission in the history books, but I swear it's all true.

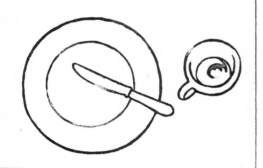

As there wasn't much to it, we finished our meal pretty quickly. We went out into the courtyard, and an officer came and told us:

The German general has surrendered.

Today, May eighth, you can say the war's over, really over, for good.

21

We rode into the village. The locals had set up tables in a field and served us an excellent breakfast, which was great because, obviously, we were still hungry.

The coffee was ersatz again, but better. There were delicious sweet rolls, nice and fresh, like Danishes, with poppy seeds on top. I love poppy seeds; when there's a lot of them, they taste like chocolate.

Listen up, guys. We have orders to go back to Pilsen. You'll be getting the itinerary. We have to avoid Prague AT ALL COSTS, because the Russians will be there.

So we went back to Pilsen. When we arrived, one of our Jeeps was missing—the one belonging to Corporal Kraus, the guy who'd boiled my machine gun.

Ten or so days later, while we were stuck waiting in two-person tents in the middle of the woods, Kraus showed up with his three men and with a big handmade American flag flying over his vehicle.

Here's their story: they'd had a flat tire, put on the spare, then got another flat. So they were stuck; they couldn't move.

Then a German vehicle showed up. It was packed with officers fleeing Prague, which the Russians had taken that very night.

They gave themselves up, happy to surrender to the Americans instead of the Russians.

Before Kraus could figure out what to do about the tire, another car arrived, full of Russians in hot pursuit of the Germans.

The Russians said to Kraus (everyone speaks some English in such circumstances):

They are your prisoners. What will you do with them?

Our corporal was no match for those Russian officers, so he said:

Okay, you can have them.

Very good.

The Russians lined them up and shot them on the spot.

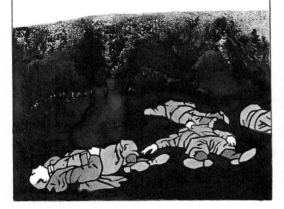

Then they replaced the tire and took our guys to Prague, where they stayed for a week, wined and dined by the Russians and Czechs.

The flag that flew over their vehicle had been sewn by Czech women, using bits of cloth.

There was once again talk of court-martialing Kraus, because he hadn't done what he should have, but in the end, the whole thing evaporated.

One day we were told a general wanted his picture taken with each of us, in thanks for our mission.

We got cleaned up, went out into a kind of field, and were introduced one by one to the general. He didn't say much, and the whole thing took place in record time.

A few days later, everybody got a copy of his photo.
No ceremony or anything, though.
The sergeant just handed them out whenever he happened to see us.
I only got mine toward the end. When he gave it to me, he said:
"Cope, here's your photo. Unfortunately, even though it says CORPORAL COPE,
I don't think it's you."
And in fact it wasn't me; it was somebody else.
I asked him: "Who is it? I'll switch."
"I don't know who that is," he answered, "but since it's all we have,
take it—at least you've got a souvenir."

I forgot about that picture for 50 years.
But recently, my younger brother—who is eighteen-and-a-half years younger than me—
sent me an old photo album he'd found in California.
In his letter, he wrote: "I was pleased to see General Patton shaking your hand.
When I lived in Pasadena, I became friends with his grandson."
It's not surprising that my brother thought it was me in the picture.
The last time we had seen each other in the flesh, he was only four years old.
I doubt it's really Patton, though.
I reckon it's a photo of a corporal who isn't Cope
shaking the hand of a general who isn't Patton.

22

Since we were going to be stationed in the suburbs of Pilsen, we requisitioned some houses. We were told of a garden nearby with an arbor, and that under the arbor there was a place where you could help yourself to a huge barrel of Pilsen beer.
So I went.

The garden was big and pretty, kind of formal like a French garden, but poorly maintained. The beer wasn't properly aged, but it was good. I like Pilsen beer. Whenever I have some I think of that place.

Strangely, most servicemen didn't go. The garden had an otherworldly feel that scared them, even though soldiers don't usually pass up on free beer. But me, I went there a lot.

Exploring the garden, I discovered it lay on the property of a beautiful home.

I was wandering alone there one day, when I met a woman.

It's hard to say how old she was. 45, maybe. She was tired, so she seemed older. She looked very aristocratic and was washing laundry in a big tub, scrubbing it by hand.

We greeted each other. She spoke German, and I knew a few words. I liked her right off the bat.

The house was hers. She wiped her hands and invited me in.

Her living room was huge, almost like a hotel lobby, with three or four sofas and a beautiful grand piano. Piles of music everywhere.

Her piano was in tune. I played very badly at the time, but she said, "Go ahead, have fun." So I picked up a score and played a bit.

Then we drank coffee. She had dark hair, and I could see that she'd been very pretty when she was young, but was careworn now.

I'm a pianist, and in my youth I gave concerts. Then the war started, and my husband died. I've been taking in laundry ever since.

She showed me her hands; they looked like the hands of a witch.

As you might imagine, I can't play anymore, because I've done all that washing in ice cold water. But I've played all the pieces that you see there.

It was heartbreaking. There, in that living room, I saw such musical beauty and accomplishment and the only way she could earn a living was by doing laundry.

I came back to see her two or three more times, always by myself. None of my fellow soldiers spoke to her. We couldn't say much because of the language barrier, but our souls were somehow akin.

And then we left for another village.

There, we stayed for a while in an abandoned manor on a riverbank. It was a big, rectangular structure, with the proportions of a slab of butter. It might have been an old Masonic building.

The house was empty, except for a few chairs. There were no fireplaces, just open spaces where wood stoves had stood. No electricity. We slept on faded wooden floors in our sleeping bags.

Downstairs, in the larger rooms, the windows were double-paned. There was a good-sized space between them, given that the walls were at least five feet thick.

When the sun was out, I liked to sit between two closed windows. It was warm, but not unpleasant. I could look out over the big park and read or write letters.

The park had a number of statues. What was weird was that none of them had been left standing.

They were reproductions of antique statues—Zeuses, Apollos, Dianas.
Some were nude, some draped. They all had been knocked over, but not broken.

Often they'd ended up in strange positions, lying face down or right-side up.
Two or three of them had fallen against a bush or a tree and stayed there, as if they were thinking or resting, maybe.

It made for a phantasmagorical, mysterious landscape, especially by moonlight.

Our billeting changed constantly.
That way, when we stayed in private houses, people weren't pushed out for too long.
It was the decent thing to do.

One evening there was a small party, with Pilsen beer and even some schnapps served by the person who lived there.
Sergeant Kubacek drank a lot.

168

It was very late and almost everyone had gone to bed. Words were exchanged, and Kubacek got mad at us.

His eyes were glassy, he called us names, and all of a sudden he pulled out a huge knife.

He didn't seem to know who we were. He became menacing, waved the knife around, said:

I'm going to kill you all.

Everyone left except me.

I didn't like Kubacek that much. I put up with him, probably in the same way he put up with me. But I said to myself: "I can't leave the guy in such a state."

It was probably the bravest thing I did during the war. I started talking to him, trying to get him to see reason. He was swaying back and forth, the knife pointed at me.

I remember that he kept growling.
I found that disturbing, but I wasn't afraid.
My only thought was,
"He has to be helped through this."

Finally I saw him melt, so to speak.
He was standing stock still, he was quiet,
his eyes weren't glassy anymore.

He mumbled something like
"good night" and left.

The next day he didn't seem to remember
anything. Exactly like Louis, the guy who
had tried to rape me.

Next we were lodged at a fairly isolated
farm. We had to stand guard 24 hours a
day in a factory. I never really understood
what kind of factory it was, even though
I spent several nights walking around.

The farm belonged to Czech Germans,
and we had humble rooms in one of its
wings. One day a dog showed up.

He was just a regular mutt. He looked like he'd come a long way, and he was hungry. Everybody was exiled at the time.

He didn't understand German or English. I spoke the two words of French I knew, but he didn't understand them either. Finally we gave him some food, and he stayed.

We were making things out of wood, both to keep busy and to build some furniture. One time Polski was building a small bench and he hit his finger hard with the hammer.

Polski was American, but, given his family background, he swore in Polish.

Immediately the dog pricked up its ears, ran over to Polski, and started yapping. He knew the swears—he was Polish.

I don't know how he'd landed there, but he was a Polish dog who understood nothing but Polish. Polski talked to him. He knew tricks. He'd give you his paw, stand on his hind legs, and do all kinds of other things, as long as you spoke his language.

In a building behind the farm lived a woman and her children.
She probably had had something to do with the factory. I don't know where the dad was.

The oldest child was about 11.
His name was Jürgen.

In time we sort of became friends. When I stood guard at night, I'd go talk to the kids in front of their house. The woman stayed inside.

Obviously they weren't dangerous. I had only a small rifle, which I'd lean against the wall when I smoked a cigarette. It was a stupid thing to do.

One evening Jürgen grabbed my loaded rifle when I wasn't looking. He shouldered it and started marching back and forth like a soldier, hup, two, hup, two.

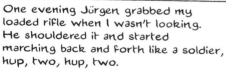

I could've kicked myself when I saw him. I said:

That's enough— give it back. You know you're not supposed to do that.

He looked at me mockingly. And then he handed me the rifle, like a good boy.

Another building was occupied by what we called displaced persons—
Gypsies from some Slavic country.
The place wasn't too bad: it had a dining room, a kitchen, an upstairs bedroom.
They could make themselves understood in English, and we'd talk.
There were two women and three men. I liked them.
I had no idea what they'd done for a living.
I could imagine the men as bartenders in a cabaret,
the women as nightclub singers or exotic dancers—
those kinds of people.
Maybe they were pimps and prostitutes.
The women were attractive, but not so young.

They had a hunting rifle. I wasn't
supposed to allow that, but I did.
They hunted rabbits and
hung them on the eaves.
They'd let the game hang
without draining the blood.
When it was nicely cured,
they'd eat it.

One day, one of the guys said to me:

Tonight we're cooking three rabbits.
Come eat with us if you like.

I managed to
get out of duty
that night and
went over.

Their cured rabbit was delicious. Really, really good. I offered them some cigarettes.

We're going to try a séance. Want to join us?

Sure.

We went upstairs. There was a round table with an alphabet all around the edge and a liquor glass on top.

We sat around the table very seriously, and they explained to me that you had to put two fingers on the base of the upside-down glass in the middle of the table, empty your thoughts, and let the glass move toward the letters.

I thought, "Well, why not give it a shot?" and I did my best to take part in the experience.

So we began, and the glass moved around quite a bit. They wrote down the letters it stopped at and shook their heads, looking dismayed. It wasn't working.

After a while and I don't know how many cigarettes, we stopped.

Nope. Not gonna work tonight.

They were really disappointed. I think they had figured that, as an American, I would contribute something extraordinary to the proceedings, but there was no message, nothing at all.

In any case, the rabbit was delicious.

We were still patrolling the countryside, going from village to village. One evening we stopped in the courtyard of a large farm where we planned to requisition some rooms.

We lined up our vehicles in the proper military way, and everyone went inside except me.

I was standing in front of our armored car, leaning against it, thinking about something. About what I don't recall.

Suddenly the vehicle lurched forward and knocked me over.

I hadn't realized that Polski was still in the car. He had decided that he wasn't quite lined up with the other vehicles. Those armored cars have a very rough clutch; when the engine starts up, they leap forward.

The front right tire started to roll over my fatigues, pinning me down. I shouted, but Polski couldn't hear me over the engine.

He was moving forward slowly, slowly, trying to line the car up properly. I couldn't pull my clothes free. The tire reached my armpit.

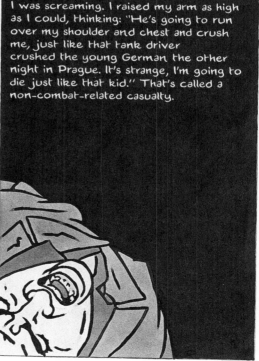

I was screaming. I raised my arm as high as I could, thinking: "He's going to run over my shoulder and chest and crush me, just like that tank driver crushed the young German the other night in Prague. It's strange, I'm going to die just like that kid." That's called a non-combat-related casualty.

He stopped.

I'd been squeezed hard, but had no injuries.

Polski got out. He came around to admire his armored-car parking skills.
He saw me under the wheel.

He was frozen in a terrible panic attack.
I managed to rip off my clothes.
I tried to comfort him.

It's okay, it's okay, I'm fine.

His shock lasted several days.
He couldn't drive. Personally, I felt fine.

23

In the village where Kubacek had pulled out a knife, where the house with the knocked-over statues was located, there flowed a beautiful river. When I think of it, I hear the music of "The Moldau," by Smetana.

It was a deep, wide river whose waters ran smooth and dark. Its banks, covered with wild grasses, sloped down steeply.

One Sunday, a village fair was held on the riverbank, a spring fair. People picnicked and played some music.

They let us attend. I went, not with my friends from the car, but with Stanley and a few others.

It was getting late, and people were starting to leave. Soon there wouldn't be anyone left. Stanley and I were walking slowly, talking and smoking cigarettes.

We came to a very big tree. Leaning against it was a Gypsy, the kind of woman you see in your dreams.

She was truly gorgeous. We gave her a cigarette, and she started to say things to me in German I didn't understand.

Stanley shook me and said:

Don't you get it? She wants you to take her home.

What? Really?

Stanley knew a bit more German than I did. Most of all, he had more experience.

You see, she's very pretty, there are men everywhere, and she's afraid to walk home alone.

"Ah," I said. "Yes."

We left. She led me out of the village.

As we gabbled at each other, neither of us understanding much, I watched her, dazzled. She was probably 16. She held my hand.

Next we took a small uphill road bordered by cut timber. She walked effortlessly, with grace and energy, like someone who could climb Mount Everest.

On the other side of the hill, we found ourselves in a very narrow valley, in a wild, forested area, on an almost non-existent little path.

We turned right, left, we went around things. I wondered: "Will I know how to get back?"

We walked for a long time. The valley grew wider and in the distance I saw a log cabin. She said: "That's where I live with my grandmother."

Suddenly she ordered:

Stop!

She pulled me to the side of the road, toward a small clearing among the pine trees where there was beautiful green grass.

Right then and there, she made it clear that she wanted me to take her.

I have to say, I was young and didn't know what to do in such moments.

She pushed me to the ground.

I said:

No.

Oh.

So we continued on toward her grandmother's log cabin.

There's no one here except my grandmother and me. The others are gone.

It was really dark by then. I wasn't allowed to be out at night, alone and without permission. I could be sanctioned. Once we got to the door, I said:

I have to go back to the village.

Come back tomorrow.

Okay—I'll come back tomorrow.

She knocked on the door and a very old woman who looked exactly like a witch— an incredible, fantastic sight— stuck her head out.

I repeated, "I'll come back tomorrow," and she said, "Yes, yes." Her grandmother grabbed her, pulled her into the house, and slammed the door.

I had to find my way back to the village, in the dark.

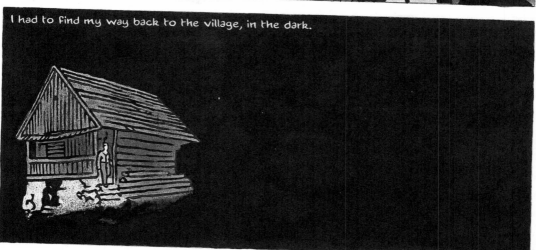

I anxiously followed all those little paths, but I didn't get it wrong.

I spent the rest of the night thinking about her. I was a callow kid.

The next day, I said to myself, "I'm going to muster up the courage and learn what love is all about."

I was able to get leave at the end of the day, and I retraced my steps.

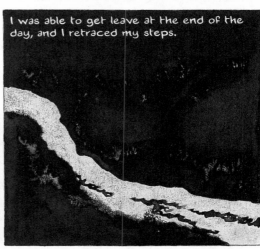

When I reached the log cabin, I knocked and knocked, but there was no answer. I looked around and called out, but no—nothing.

They were gone.

I've put myself
in a pretty pathetic light,
telling that story.
But so what?
It's not that bad.
I can still see that Gypsy,
her incredible beauty,
her long skirt
and her long hair,
living in the middle of the woods
with her grandmother.
It's... HAHAHA!
It's unbelievable.
The story didn't end too well.

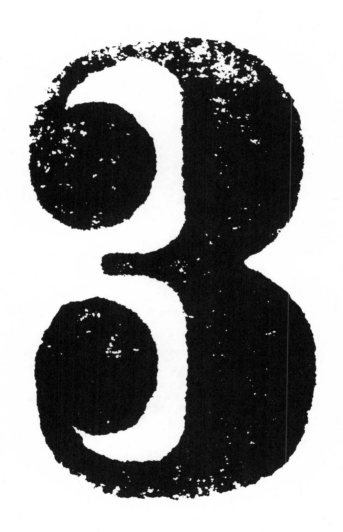

24

My unit was stationed in the forests of Bohemia, near Marienbad.
Sometimes, in the evening, I'd go into Marienbad.

There I met a very young German boy named Jako. He was maybe nine or ten years old. The Americans had picked him up, adopted him, and made him a little uniform. He was from some city in Poland, I don't remember which one. He had no family at all.

He spoke English.

Listen, you can't just stay here. Do you want to come to America with me?

Okay, Shorty.

He called me Shorty. I wasn't very tall.

I wrote to my parents, but they didn't answer. I went to see the chaplain, I made some other inquiries, but no luck.

Suddenly, we had to leave Czechoslovakia at once because of the Yalta accords. We left in a rush, and I lost track of him.

I ended up in Germany, right near the city of Regensburg, formerly Ratisbon.

I was a radio operator, and since my skills were no longer needed, I was always on guard duty. It was boring, and winter was coming.

One day, the administrative officer who did all the typing—the company clerk—left. The war was over, and more and more soldiers were being sent home.
It was getting harder to find people with specialized skills.
At morning roll call, they asked us:

Does anyone know how to type?

I thought, "I'm sick and tired of guard duty," so I said:

I do.

I could type a little.

Well, it turned out to be exhausting work. It was all transfers. There were people coming in from all over and others going back to America. It was endless. I worked from morning till very late at night.

Sometimes, though, I managed to go into town. German musicians played in the makeshift mess hall.

One lunchtime, I noticed a brother and sister singing Bavarian songs, accompanying themselves on the accordion: Klementine and Erich. She was barely 16, he barely 18.

They were really cute, and played and sang well. We struck up a kind of friendship, as best we could in our different languages.

They ended up inviting me to their house, with their parents' permission.

They lived in a small house in old Ratisbon; the address was 1 Kuhgässel, meaning Cow Lane. Their street was so narrow that, legend has it, a pregnant cow once got stuck there and had to give birth on the spot, right between the two walls, because she couldn't move at all.

I can believe it; even a person could only just squeeze through.

191

When they opened the door, I saw two buildings and a small courtyard garden with a tree. On the left stood a shed, and the main house, on the right. There was an arbor in back and, in the rear, a sort of barnyard with geese and a few hens.

I met Ma and Pa Rossbauer. He was a trolley driver. A family friend lived with them, who they called Uncle Peppi. We were served an outstanding gourmet meal.

I learned that Erich and Klementine were actually only cousins.

Erich is my sister's son. She died young, when he was nine. I raised him with my own children.

My son's name is Helmut. He's 22 and in a prison camp, luckily not too far away. He was in a tank unit, like you. Four years of war and not a scratch on him, and then, a month before it ends, he gets his left leg torn off.

The Rossbauers often invited me back. In fact, they gave me an open invitation to eat with them anytime, so I went whenever I could. I started learning German.

1 Kuhgäffel (A 132½)

I have to admit, I found Klementine very attractive, but my conscience troubled me.

For the past few weeks I had been corresponding with Patzi, Egypt's sister, and we were basically falling in love through letters.
That was a mistake, by the way, but I didn't find that out till later.

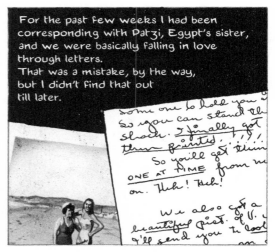

Klementine sang for me and started to knit me a beautiful jacquard sweater. I guess you could say things were starting to get kind of serious.

We went to see Helmut at the prison camp during visiting hours. He was wearing long pants, with the empty leg tied up at the cuff with a rubber band. I'd shove a whole bunch of cigarettes and chocolate into his pocket, which he'd torn open, and the leg would fill up just like a sack.

I brought them whatever I could—me, the American who had everything—but I have to admit, it was really them who spoiled me.
Ma Rossbauer had family in the country, near Regensburg.
She'd go visit them and come back with things to eat.
She made jam and strawberry and raspberry liqueurs.
She had a trick, which she never revealed to me, for keeping eggs fresh for months.
I never went down into her cellar, but marvelous treats emerged from it.

One day I was walking around Regensburg and heard:

Hey, Shorty! Is that you?

JAKO!

What are you doing here?

Not much. Whatever I can.

I was delighted to see Jako again.

He was wearing civilian clothes, and there was something crass about him—the way he looked, and spoke.

Listen, I'm going to see some friends—why don't you come along? You can eat and sleep there, if you want.

Sounds good.

The Rossbauers welcomed him warmly, and he stayed overnight. The next day Klementine complained:

He's so rude! He talks like a... You can't imagine!!

Jako told me he'd forgiven me for not taking him along when I'd left Marienbad.

I'll manage. I know how to do all sorts of things.

He walked away; I never saw him again.

25

All of a sudden I was transferred. Our unit chaplain, Pliney Elliot, had just lost his assistant, who'd returned to the States.

Would you like to be my assistant? I hear you can play the organ and sing well.

I can manage on the harmonium, but I'm not a good singer.

I wasn't keen to leave Regensburg.

Do you know how to drive?

No—well, I can drive a tank, but a car, not really.

Ah! That's a problem.

You don't know how to drive either?

Yes, but I hate it. Oh well, you'll learn. I'll sort out the transfer with your chief administrative officer. We're leaving tomorrow.

The following afternoon I found myself sitting behind the wheel of a Jeep with a trailer in tow, driving toward the Alps with Chaplain Elliot by my side.

Night soon fell, and it started to snow. He navigated while I drove as best I could.

He made a few mistakes, so I'd have to back up, with my trailer, along narrow, unlit roads.
Two or three times I almost hit cars coming right at us.

When the road wasn't too treacherous, he'd talk. He was about 45, from the Midwest–Kansas City. A very fundamentalist type, but that didn't bother me. I was, too, at the time. He was a genuinely sincere man.

A few months ago, I saw them liberate a concentration camp near Munich. I was one of the first soldiers to arrive.

Outside the camp, near the entrance, there was a horse that had obviously been dead for days. It had a huge, bloated stomach and its legs were sticking straight up in the air. When we opened the gates, the few starving prisoners who were still able to run threw themselves onto that horse and started eating it raw.

He kept talking. He was obviously distraught, and so was I.

We headed into mountain roads.
The good lord took pity on his chaplain, and we didn't have an accident.
My companion talked about his wife, sang her praises.
I found him impressive, both gentle and strong. That's a rare combination.

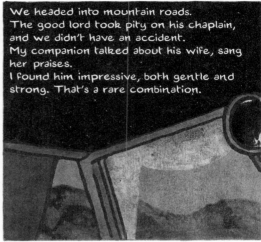

In the wee hours of the morning, we came to a faintly lit village.

We're here. Go straight, to where you'll be staying.

Stop—this is it.

I had learned to drive in one night.
I was pleased with myself, and so was he.

I'll have a serviceman park the Jeep. Grab your things, settle in, and get some rest.

Okay, thanks.

An NCO ushered me into a big chalet.

How are you? Let me show you around, you can choose a room.

No one had spoken to me that kindly since the beginning of the war. I was more used to diabolical NCOs.

I've got two or three empty ones. You can take a look at them and pick the room you want.

This one has a balcony.

I'll take it.

I fell asleep thinking: "You've landed in heaven."

When I woke up, it was early afternoon. I opened the balcony window.

When I came down afterward, the NCO told me that the lake was called the Tegernsee and the town Bad Wiessee. We were in the southern tip of Bavaria, near the Austrian border.

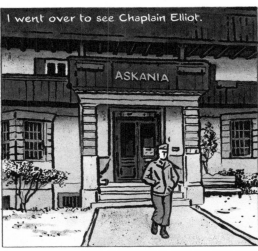

I went over to see Chaplain Elliot.

ASKANIA

He was taking up his functions as chaplain in a large hotel that had been turned into a field hospital.

He showed me the vast, beautiful dining room, which had a huge white ceramic stove in the middle and bay windows overlooking the mountains.

I had a great time there, staying six months. Six unbelievable months.

26

We traveled to all sorts of small towns. I'd set up the altar, play the harmonium, and lead the servicemen in song. Nothing too hard.

The chaplain, being from the Midwest, liked hunting and owned a gun.
We'd head for the fields, where he would direct me and shoot from the Jeep.

I picked up whatever dropped to the ground. We came back with an incalculable number of birds, and on Sunday we'd eat pheasant in the mess hall. He also gave some to the Germans, who weren't allowed to have firearms and couldn't hunt.

Sometimes we had to travel really far afield, all the way to Nuremberg, to a camp for displaced Slavs. We'd bring wine for the mass, candles, Bibles, and German and Slavic-language literature to a Catholic priest named Rudi.

It was a really long trip, so we'd stop over in Regensburg for the night.

I had told the chaplain about my friends the Rossbauers. It turned out he knew Klementine and Erich.

Are they the two who play the accordion in the mess hall?

Yeah, and they sing, too.

You can drop me off at the hotel for traveling officers. Their servicemen's quarters aren't great, though. Since you have a standing invitation at your friends' house, you'd be better off rooming with them.

Okay, thanks!

There's only one problem: you're not allowed to leave the Jeep outside. And if you put it in the parking lot, you won't be able to leave the barracks.

I'll think of something.

The truth is, it was forbidden to fraternize with the Germans. But, of course, I fraternized as much as I could, as I've done all my life, wherever I end up.

The Rossbauers were thrilled to see me. Right away, Ma Rossbauer had a plan for the Jeep.

Come with me.

Right next to the Kuhgässel stood a church that had been turned into an orphanage. Ma Rossbauer was friends with the nuns who ran it. They opened up the big gates, and I parked the Jeep in the cloister. No harm, no foul.

My one-night parking spot cost me three gallons of gasoline. The nuns needed it to make wax polish. No problem, though. We Americans could have as much as we liked.

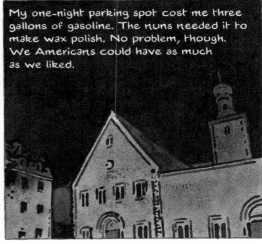

The next day, at dawn, I quietly fetched the Jeep from the church and picked up the chaplain at his hotel; then we left for Nuremberg. We used that system a few times, and it worked well.

We had to go to Nuremberg quite often, because Rudi, the Catholic priest, conducted a lot of masses in several local churches, so he needed a lot of wine and other supplies.

One day we found him drunk. Chaplain Elliot got him to admit that, in fact, he said very few masses, but drank the wine, and even sold some of it. The chaplain gave him a well-deserved dressing-down.

The chaplain had trusted the man. Personally, I'd never liked him. Some con men are nice people, but all in all that's pretty rare. We'd come with a lot of bottles, but we left him only one.

That should be enough for your masses until I come back.

Thanks to the network of American military chaplains, we were warmly welcomed in all kinds of places. Along with nurses from the hospital, we were given private tours of Ludwig II's castles—which were closed at the time—and of Richard Strauss's house in Partenkirchen.

Once, in Regensburg, I spoke to the Rossbauers about the snow-covered mountains that surrounded Lake Tegernsee. As a young Californian who had never skied, I wanted to try it.

Well, I've got skis!

Would you rent them to me?

The skis were much too long for me, but Erich decided it didn't matter. He gave me the matching poles.

At Bad Wiessee, I met up with an old military buddy, a jock in charge of the hospital staff's basketball team. He had borrowed a pair of skis and, like me, hadn't ever skied.

We have to find a nice little slope where no one can see us and give it our best.

One night, when the sky was bright from the full moon, we climbed a hill at the edge of the village. The snow was well packed and slippery.

We drew straws to see who'd go down first. He won and went ahead.

I kept a reasonable distance behind him, on my overly long skis. I could just about manage.

I found him at the bottom of the slope, sprawled on the ground.

I broke my leg.

I had to drag him over to the road. He was a heavy guy.

Luckily, we didn't have to wait too long.
A passing patrol took him to the hospital.

The basketball team lost all its games that season.

A few days later, I took a walk on that same slope with another soldier, Jim Post, who was a bit older than me.

As we chatted, a couple passed by— a man and woman in their forties. They came over, and started politely talking to us.

That's how I met this man who was— I say was because he's dead now— a truly extraordinary individual: GERHART MUENCH.

27

We soon became fast friends. Gerhart was a German composer and pianist:
Vera, his wife, an American poet from Boston.
They were renting the first floor of a small house in Bad Wiessee.

There was almost nothing in it
except a typewriter and a piano.
They served us tea; we brought them
cigarettes and a few bottles of wine.
And Gerhart played.

Jim Post and I spent unforgettable hours
listening to a REAL pianist. He played
all sorts of things, a lot of Chopin and
Brahms. He also played some Scriabin, a
discovery for me.

Gerhart's story is a long one.
Our paths continued to
cross, all over the world,
in a strange kind of way.
You'll see.
I really liked him.

He was born in Dresden in 1907. He'd been a child
prodigy: he knew Latin, Greek, some Hebrew, and five
or six modern languages. At 20, like so many young
Germans in his social and artistic circle, he did some
traveling and went to Paris to live the good life.

Physically he was fairly unattractive, almost ugly. But he was passionate about love, and women liked him a lot. He kept a Parisian mistress, married to a Polish painter. She lived at 45, rue du Faubourg Saint-Honoré. Her name was Bettina.

He stayed in Paris for ten years, leading an easy life. He was always able to make money playing the piano. He knew a lot of people, including the Belgian playwright Fernand Crommelynck, author of "The Magnificent Cuckold"—a good play, that. They were close friends.

After ten years,
he thought:
"I'm wasting my life away,
doing nothing.
I have to leave."

He took off for Italy.

There he wandered around the northern part of the country, supporting himself by playing the piano wherever he could. He met the poet Ezra Pound and spent three years with him. Pound was not an easygoing kind of guy.

In his "Canto de Pisa 75,"
Pound mentions Gerhart:
"Out of Phlegethon!
Out of Phlegethon,
Gerhart
Art thou come forth out of Phlegethon?
With Buxtehude and Klages in your satchel, with the Ständebuch of Sachs in your luggage—not of one bird but of many."
In the version I have, there are a few lines of text and two pages of music. The music, of course, is by Gerhart. I had a copy blown up so I could try to play it myself.

Here it is.

LXXV

Out of Phlegethon!
out of Phlegethon,
Gerhart
art thou come forth out of Phlegethon?
with Buxtehude and Klages in your satchel, with the
Ständebuch of Sachs in yr/ luggage
—not of one bird but of many

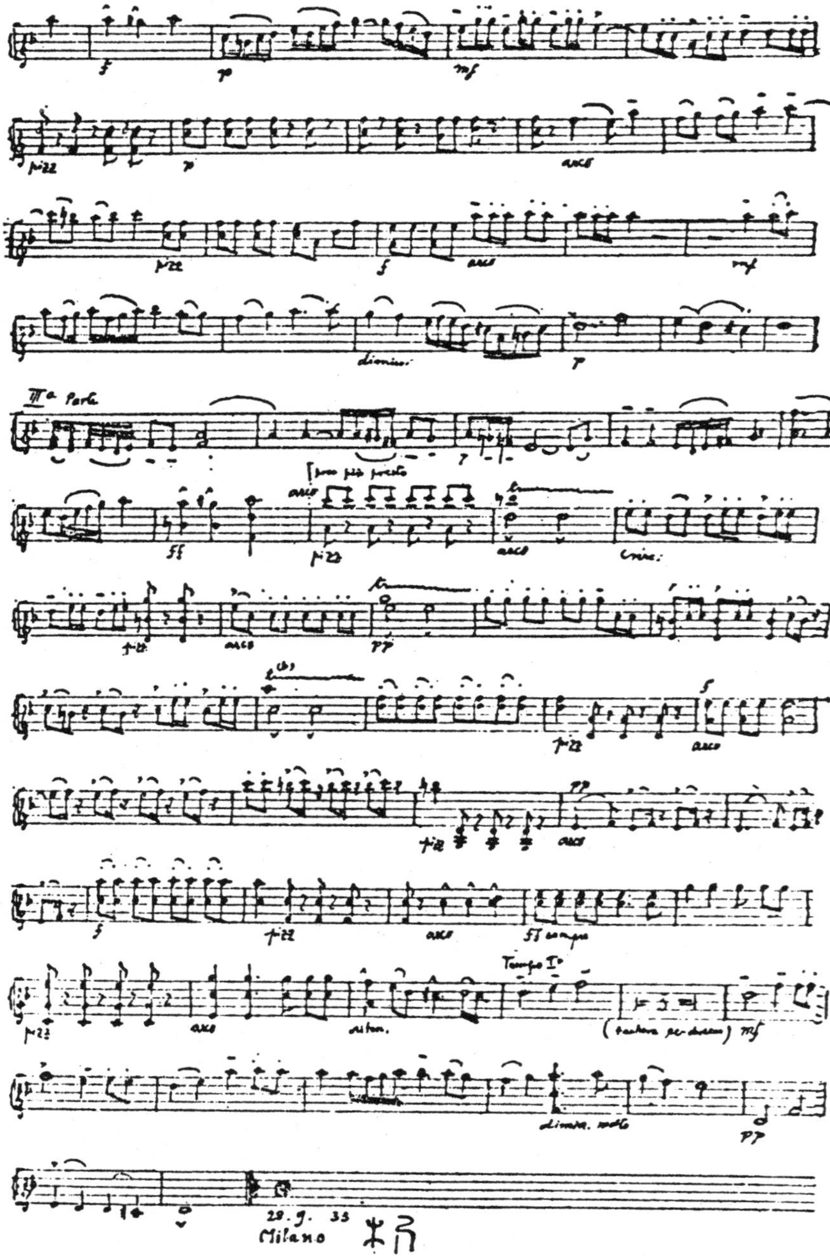
pizz
arco
IIIa Parte
cresc.
ff sempre
Tempo I°
28.9.33
Milano

The poem mentions Ludwig Klages,
an author Gerhart liked.
He's best known as the father
of handwriting analysis, but I think
he was really more of a philosopher.

According to Gerhart and Vera,
Klages wrote two important
books, both almost impossible to find.
One long and one short.
The first is called:
"Vom Wesen des Bewusstseins,"
which I believe can be translated as
"On the Awareness of Being."

Vera told me she'd borrowed that
book when she was a student at the
University of Vienna. It became so
important to her, because she couldn't
afford to buy it she copied out over a
thousand pages by hand.

I tried to get my hands on a volume.
A book dealer told me that his son,
a Munich bookseller, could find me one,
but that fell through.

The second, smaller book is called
"Von kosmogoniche Eros,"
or "Cosmic Eros."

Years ago, I borrowed it from France's
La Rochelle municipal library; it came
from the Sorbonne in Paris and was
on loan to me for a month.
I typed it out as well as I could, hardly
understanding a word (it's written
in difficult German), and when I ran out of
time, I had the last few pages photocopied.

I still haven't read it.
I'd promised myself I would
read it someday.

Ezra Pound wrote extraordinary poems, but he was so wrong about many things. He urged Americans to desert during the war. It's interesting looking at his life as a sort of lesson in error.
A lot of artists made the mistake of becoming fascists.

Richard Strauss, for instance, was blacklisted by the Americans for a short while after the war. Gerhart, who'd met him in the 1930s, said:
"That man knew nothing but music. He should have kept his big mouth shut when it came to politics, about which he understood nothing."

Gerhart eventually landed in Capri, a popular spot at the time for people like him. That's where he met Vera. Vera's family was one of the wealthiest in Boston, having made a fortune in glassware manufacturing. But Vera, like Gerhart, had turned her back on her family's expectations and didn't have a penny to her name.

Extraordinarily, because it was totally out of character for them, they decided to get married. Their friends tried to talk them out of it.

It's a stupid idea. People like us just don't get married. You'll be divorced within three days.

No—we're getting married.

Then Gerhart wanted to return to Dresden to settle some family business.
His friends were up in arms.

Are you completely mad? You can't go back to Germany! You have no idea what things are like with Hitler there! Neither of you will make it out alive!

Bah! It's just for a couple of weeks. We'll be heading right back.

They were stuck in Germany for the entire war.

Gerhart got drafted. They wanted him to play the piano for Nazi officers, but he refused. He was never one to compromise—he'd rather die first.
I've never known anyone else as steadfast as Gerhart.

As an American citizen, Vera was encouraged to return to the United States. She refused.

I'm staying with my husband.

They assigned Gerhart to a construction unit that fixed roofs in the dead of winter—a terrible thing for a pianist's hands.

Vera battled with the local High Command until she finally got them to see that they were sacrificing a German artist for absurd reasons. She also persuaded Gerhart to play not for the officers, but for the enlisted men.

So he played for the soldiers. That's how he saved his hands, maybe even his life, but it was devastating for him. The whole time I knew him, he suffered from serious bouts of depression.

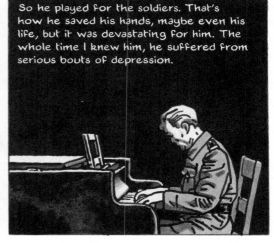

They lived through the terrible firebombing of Dresden.
They'd been staying with an uncle. Gerhart used to cite him as a model of German stupidity.
When things got really bad, they'd all go down to the cellar.
But the uncle insisted on winding up his living room clock before going to safety.

He could have died winding that clock.

Anyway, they survived and ended up on the shores of the Tegernsee, where I met them. At the time of their arrival, Patton had one of his homes on the other side of the lake.

As headquarters was short on typewriters, Patton had every one in the area seized, including Vera's.

She went to him personally and said:

I too am an American citizen, and as you know, my husband is an honorable man. And yet you take from me my only valuable possession? My source of comfort, and means for a living?

She got her typewriter back. That's the kind of woman Vera was.

212

28

And then there was a girl called Gisela.
She was my age and worked for the American army as a telephone operator.
The High Command had okayed her for that job, despite the fact that her father had been a general in the Wehrmacht, though not a Nazi.
She was blonde, pretty as a picture, and very smart. We became friends— or buddies, at least.
The others didn't like her.
They called her "Cope's nasty little Nazi."
I have to admit, it's true she'd believed in Nazism.
She was sorry it hadn't worked out.

She introduced me to her mother and sister, who was two years younger than her. Her mom was one of those terribly proper German women, very shy and retiring. Her father had died on the Russian front. On the mantelpiece sat an urn full of soil from his grave.
Next to it was a condolence letter signed by Adolf Hitler.

They wouldn't take anything from me, except for a few cigarettes for Gisela. Every time I came by I'd get a couple of slices of toast slathered in lard, because there wasn't any butter.

When my father died, my mother and sister left Berlin. I decided to stay.

I wanted to stay till the end.

Finally, at the end of March, a friend of my father's was able to get me onto the last civilian train out of Berlin, and I agreed to go. But I loathed the idea of it. It felt like deserting.

As the train started moving, a woman on the platform tossed a baby through an open window and into my arms, crying: "Please save my son!"

I thought: "Here I am, just 20 years old. I could never show my face at home, coming back with a baby." I did the best I could with him for a few hours.

Luckily, later on in the trip his mother, who'd finally managed to get on the train, came and took him off my hands.

One time I persuaded Gisela to go to a dance with me at the American center. She told me: "The idea of going to an American dance is disgusting." But she did it anyway.

G.I. GARDEN
MUSIC
BEER
girlfriends invited
OFF LIMITS
TO OFFICERS

On top of her job as a telephone operator, to earn some money she tutored the local children in math, Latin, and French. One of her students was a very nice 15-year-old war orphan named Christoph.

One evening, after his lesson, he stayed quite late talking to us (I was there, too). We lost track of time.

Back then, there was a strict curfew because of the Werewolves, roving bands of young Germans crushed by their country's defeat, who'd become terrorists.
They were dangerous and came out mainly at night.

Christoph lived in the woods with his aunt. He was a bit too young to go home by himself.

Would you come with me? We can take him home together.

Okay.

As a soldier, I was taking a big risk by breaking curfew, especially since the skiing incident, which I'd already been punished for.

We slipped out and headed for the woods.

We passed two American patrols and managed to get around them without being seen.

That's when I realized how good the Hitler Youth training had been, because Gisela was amazing, crawling through the forest on her stomach. She basically directed the whole maneuver.

We dropped Christoph off and came back the same way. Once she was home, I returned to my place. HAHAHA! Yes, I did things no American soldier ever should.

Christoph was quite proud of having an American friend. He sent me two letters much later. The first one included a picture. He'd become a waiter in a very fancy hotel in the Swiss Alps and was decked out in a stylish uniform.

In the second letter, he wrote:
"I'm an international bartender on a cruise ship. I've discovered women and whiskey, and I'm very happy."

In '58, in Poitiers, I lost my address book. With that, I lost Christoph.

One day, Gisela said to me:

Well, I've now got 50 pounds of potatoes in a sack—it's time for me to hitchhike to Heidelberg to continue my studies.

So she left.
The potatoes would be her food for a while, because there was nothing to eat.

Life was strange, you know.
And so was Gisela.

In mid-March 1946, the captain who was our hospital administrator told me I was going to be demobilized and could go back to the States; that would be the end of my military service.
He added:

I need an assistant, though, and I'd like you to stay on as a civilian employee.

That was something new.

In the meantime, getting to know the chaplain had made me want to be a minister.
I was making a mistake, but I didn't know that then.
I thought:
"I have to go back to America and take advantage of the G.I. bill to go to college. I have to start living an ordinary American life, marry Patzi, become a minister, and save the souls of sinners."

So I said:

Thanks, but I can't.
I have to go home.

A week later, on March 22, I was supposed to go to headquarters, in Bad Tölz, to get my demobilization certificate.
It was about a 12-mile journey from Bad Wiessee—the first leg of my return trip.

I had packed up my belongings and said good-bye to everyone the night before. Around 7 a.m., I woke up in that nice little room I loved, and thought:

Cope, you're making a stupid mistake.

I called the captain right away.

Does the offer still stand? Because I've changed my mind. I'd like to take you up on it.

Glad to hear it. Take a Jeep, go to Bad Tölz to get your papers, and come straight back. I'll call them right away so they can register you as a civilian worker.

So in the end, I did the right thing. I got a renewable six-month contract and they gave me that strangest of things—a civilian employee's uniform.

After two weeks, the captain sent me to a small branch of our hospital, in Sonthofen, near Obertsdorf in the Allgäu region. Paradise. It's the southernmost tip of Germany.

29

I was housed in a wing that had been requisitioned for the hospital's doctors and nurses. They weren't very nice people, and in fact looked down on me. The minister wasn't so great either.

Young German Christians came to the American service on Sundays. The minister decided to form a kind of club, and a leader needed to be elected. We had to explain to them how to do it. They obviously had no idea what a vote was.

At the hospital I met a German electrician. He was maybe 16. He had a slightly younger friend who was a hairdresser and another, even younger friend. All three had been born in the valley and worked for the Americans.

We soon became friends. One day they said to me:

We can take you up into the mountains, if you want.

That'd be great!

The following Saturday night I closed up the hospital, as I did every night. I had all the keys.

I went into the kitchen to steal some food—some meat, a can of this and that. Not much, just enough to feed us. I would've gladly bought it, but at that hour, it was impossible.

At 3 a.m., as planned, I heard the three of them whistle for me.
I climbed out my bedroom window, which faced the tracks of the little Allgäu railway line.

We left in the dark and headed for the nearby mountains.

That Sunday, all day until past midnight, we made one amazing climb after another.
They knew the mountains inside out and taught me mountain hiking.

We started doing that every Sunday. The nurses and doctors I lived with had no idea where I went. I'd stopped going to religious services.
I'd just disappear.

My buddies took me to a number of beautiful places—small lakes and summer pastures.

Once we went as far as the Austrian border on four bicycles they'd borrowed, where from I have no idea. They were old bikes, without brakes.

The idea was to go down certain hills as fast as possible, sometimes dragging our feet to slow ourselves down.
It was terrifying and wonderful.

Most important, they taught me how to go down mountains like a goat, by hopping. It's an amazing technique. You can cover in 20 minutes what it took you 3 hours to climb, but you do need good hiking shoes.

One time we took Kinney with us. You remember Kinney? I talked about him earlier. He was that nice guy I'd offered my pillaged watch to.

We discovered he was afraid of heights. During the more difficult bits he'd say: "Oh! I can't believe it! It's so beautiful! I want to go there! I want to go there!" And so he would, crawling on all fours.

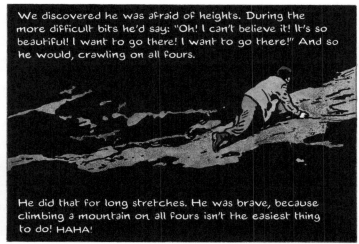

He did that for long stretches. He was brave, because climbing a mountain on all fours isn't the easiest thing to do! HAHA!

Almost 30 years later, in the early '70s, I went back to Sonthofen with my wife. We lived in Germany at the time.
Before our trip, I'd asked a friend to place a few classified ads in the local papers to try to locate those three guys.
I would've really liked to find them again! But it didn't work out. Too bad.

Once, during my stay in Allgäu, I went to Bad Wiessee. I visited Gerhart and Vera, who were pretty downcast. They were drinking too much.

I also saw Gisela's mother.

Things have changed with Gisela; she's getting married. I'll show you a photo.

She's marrying this Russian prince who's in Munich right now. That's the two of them with the prince's retinue, 18 people.

They're going to live in South America. Here, take it. I've got others.

Thanks.

Since then, I've heard lots of stories about Nazis fleeing to South America, and I suspect she was helping a Nazi escape. He might really have been a Russian prince, because some of them were very much pro-Hitler. I lost that little picture, and I wish I hadn't. I'd love to look at all those people again.

The six months of my contract went by quickly. I'd continued writing to Patzi and, for reasons that were basically religious and just plain stupid, we'd gotten engaged by letter. I decided to return to the States.
I should have stayed where I was. I was very happy, and I could've had a nice, completely different little career.

I stopped one last time in Bad Wiessee before leaving Germany. I said good-bye to Gerhart and Vera and gave them my address in America—733 Highland Street, Pasadena, California—and we promised to keep in touch.

This time Gisela's mother handed me a postcard addressed to me— no envelope—obviously hastily written and mailed from Munich.

It was a picture of an eagle with its wings spread, a very nice one, the kind of thing you find in zoos. On the back was written, in English: "Dear Alan, the eagle has spread its wings. Gisela"

That was typical of her, and it meant just what it said: she was leaving for good.

That was the end of my stay in the Alps.

30

So I came back to the States. I arrived in New York, headed for California. First, I went to see Lou. He lived in New Jersey, on the other side of the river. It would have been unthinkable to be so close and not go see him.

Lou introduced me to his family and his fiancée. Quite seriously, he said to me:

Stay with us. My brother and I are going to build houses. We could all go into business together.

Maybe I should have, who knows? I doubt it, though.

I also stopped over in Kansas City to see Chaplain Elliot. He was happy to see me. His wife was there, and I remembered all the nice things he'd said about her. She was about 15 years younger than him. A real beauty, with long black hair. She was demure and dignified, but could easily have been a pin-up in a magazine.

He was basically the one who'd inspired me to become a minister. Some believers have a real strength in them.

Finally, I arrived in California.

I met my fiancée. I knew Egypt very well, but Patzi, not so much. Things didn't go too badly, except that Egypt didn't at all like the idea of my getting engaged to her sister.

It wasn't jealousy (she herself was about to get married); it was just that she didn't think I was the husband for Patzi.
She was right, too. It wasn't a good idea.

I had an old jalopy, a '34 Chevy, a two-seater with a rumble seat that my dad had fixed up. I'd take Patzi to Santa Barbara for the day —a 200-mile trip in all
We'd take the old road, the Camino Real.

There was a place we liked to eat on the way back, a two-story inn in the middle of nowhere with a restaurant downstairs and a small parking lot, all of it shaded by a single oak tree with branches fanning out overhead. It was beautiful.

I suppose it's long gone by now, but it's still there in my memory.

One time we had an accident, Patzi, her parents, and I. Her dad was driving.

He opened the door to spit (his car was one of those old Lincolns where the doors opened front to back). The wind surprised him, knocked him off balance.

He let go of the wheel and the car swerved onto the shoulder. He made the mistake of trying to straighten it out.

The car rolled over several times.

My face hit the ceiling—hard—again and again.

The four of us ended up in a little country hospital, a clinic, really. My face was covered in bruises.

Patzi and her parents got out the next day, but not me. They kept me there for four days, flat on my back without a pillow.

The doctor didn't have an X-ray machine and suspected brain trauma. I couldn't stand it any more.

Doctor, when can I leave?

We're keeping you under observation for now.

Your pulse is only 40 this morning.

In that case you're going to have to keep me here for years. My morning pulse is always 40.

My dad confirmed that over the phone, and I was discharged.

HOSPITAL

Even today, I still have a marathon runner's pulse.

I got into the University of Redlands (it's between Los Angeles and Palm Springs), thanks to the G.I. Bill. Without it, I wouldn't have been able to afford going back to school.
Redlands had a good reputation for training future Baptist ministers.

I drove back to Pasadena each weekend, and the cost was really adding up. Things were tight, and I had to get a job on the side.

I started out by helping a rich kid with his homework—probably, let's see, maybe 12 years old tops. I went there twice a week, but it didn't pay much. The poor kid was totally spoiled. He lived in the middle of his parents' huge orange grove, in a really modern house.

They had nice things, but all the carpets—just to give you an idea of how stupidly nouveau rich they were—were thick and white as snow. And when I say white, I mean WHITE. Lily white. Of course, they had a maid who spent all her time cleaning them.

My little student didn't have a room—he had a suite. First there was a kind of living room, then an office, with an adjoining bathroom and workshop. He suffered from every imaginable complex. He wasn't at all cooperative; he was a real basket case.

I quickly realized that I couldn't do anything for him, because he didn't want my help. And so, since they weren't paying me much, I quit.

I passed him on to another student, who later said to me:

I'm working him hard, and we're starting to see some results. But he's really terrible. You have to be extremely tough with him.

I found another job in a local house run by a minister. It had two rooms and a small playground in the back for the poor Mexican kids from the neighborhood.

It was basically empty, just a few benches and a bare table. Luckily, the weather in California is almost always nice, so the kids could play soccer or horseshoes outside.

The minister was a completely useless man. He knew nothing about how to look after children because he didn't like having them around. The good lord made a mistake when he chose that man to be a minister. I guess he knew how to pray, but that was it.

I'd go there once in a while during the week and open the place up for an hour. Six or seven young Mexicans would show up, no more than that. Four of them were real regulars.

I thought: "I really should get them to do something." I told the four them:

I have a car. Why don't I take you guys for a hike in the mountains?

Boy, that really made them happy.

Bring a sandwich if you can. I'll try to scrounge up something, too. And, most importantly, ask your parents' permission.

Our parents couldn't care less what we do.

We set out on a Saturday morning. I had one of them next to me and three in the back, in the rumble seat.

I took them up into a really wild area, on a tiny road I'd discovered by accident.

Of course, they were undisciplined and I had to watch them every second, but everything went well.
We clambered up ravines and climbed trees. I took pictures.

They came back thrilled, and we became pretty close after that. Later, when I returned to Europe, the oldest wrote to me. He always said how memorable that day had been for him. His name was Tony.

231

I made a few good friends at Redlands. One of them was Flint.

Flint was very religious. He worried a lot because he was poor, and suddenly he had a nervous breakdown.
That was the first time I'd seen anyone have one.
He was put in the university clinic to rest.

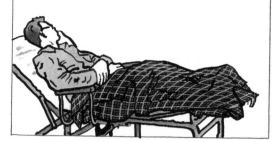

One day he introduced me to Landis—the opposite of Flint.
He had money, a nice little car, and his father paying for a comfortable room in town, with a private entrance.
He was four years younger than me, so he hadn't been drafted and had escaped the war.

Landis had really thick lips, but they suited him. His face could handle it. He didn't have a girlfriend. He told me that a nymphomaniac was chasing him and that he couldn't get rid of her. It was pretty funny.
I liked him a lot. He HATED religion. He couldn't understand why I wanted to be a minister. Because of that we hardly ever spoke about it.
He was fairly intellectual, very pleasant, without a violent bone in his body. He was one of those people who do no harm.
He listened to Baroque music and was a poet. By that I mean he was a talented writer; he wanted to do it for a living.

232

In addition to our humanities core curriculum, he was taking elective classes in creative writing and psychology. I was taking a psychology course, too.

One subject I couldn't get enough of, even though I knew nothing about it, was American and British poetry. Landis taught me a lot about that. I still have an anthology of modern English poets with his check marks in the index, and his comments as he went along:

You can read that, that's good.

That's good too.

And that.

I remember that one of his favorite American poets was e.e. cummings.

One day a large tent went up, for some ministers who were going to hold a big, old-style Christian prayer meeting. The center aisle was covered in sawdust, and people would march up to the altar to give their soul to the Lord, saying "I believe" and all that sort of thing.

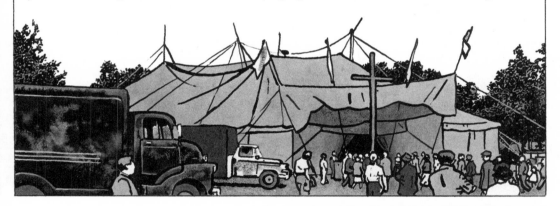

It was very dramatic and, truth be told, I took it all pretty seriously, even though I didn't particularly like the showmanship involved. I brought Landis along because I wanted him to see this strange thing.

Well, even though Landis was a polite kid, he couldn't stop cracking up.

I spent a weekend with his family in Coronado, at San Diego Bay, just north of the Mexican border. It was all money over there. His father had already retired. He'd been a ship's captain. That's a very high rank in the merchant marines—equivalent to general in the army. Those people make big bucks.

I stayed in a guesthouse in the garden. I had a bedroom, a bathroom, a living room, and even a desk with everything you could need to write—stationery, envelopes, stamps and such.
Landis said to me: "Dad likes people in the guesthouse to have absolutely everything they need."

In the evening, by the fire, we had drinks before dinner. His dad was really nice, a great guy. Having just spent three years in the army, I had great respect for him. At one point Landis said to him:

Dad, you should sing a song for Alan.

Okay, if you want. Which one?

The telephone.

So he got up and sang for me:

I just called up to tell you that I'm ragged but right

A thievin' gamblin' woman and I'm drunk ev'ry night

I eat a porterhouse steak three times a day for my board

More than any self-respecting gal can afford

I got a big electric fan to keep me cool when I sleep

I got a big and handsome man to play around with my feet

Oh, I'm a thievin' woman, gamblin' woman, I'm drunk ev'ry niiiiight...

I just called up to tell you that I'm RAGGED but right!

You get the picture, don't you? It was pretty unexpected.

At the beginning of my second semester, Stanford University, in Palo Alto, just south of San Francisco, launched a special program for students who wanted to study Jesus's teachings in depth, to then go implement them in society. The people in charge looked interesting, and so did the location: the redwood forests on the coast between San Francisco and Big Sur.

I applied. Flint approved, Landis didn't.

What on earth are you going to do there, stuck in the middle of those forests, besides wasting your time?

He was leaving to continue his studies in Berkeley.

I was admitted. Redlands granted me a three-month sabbatical, and I left.

235

31

You can't imagine the effect that those coastal California redwoods can have on you unless you've seen them yourself. Photographs don't do them justice. They're truly giant trees. It's like being on another planet.

There were about 30 people in our group. The seminar was worthwhile, made you think. The discussions were useful.
I remember one of them was on the topic: "We have to replace the idea that 'the end justifies the means,' with the thought that 'the means determine the end.'"

We did interpretive dance, which was a lot of fun. In a group setting and that kind of atmosphere, it was quite a surprising sensation.

Sometimes I'd play the harmonium.

The undergrowth was incredibly green and lush. The ferns were so high, you could walk under them.

In our free time, I'd walk all alone, far into the forest. I'd keep looking up but couldn't see where the trees ended. It was amazing.

One day I came across something strange: two rows of four redwoods each, perfectly straight and parallel. It was an accident, because those forests weren't planted. A straight line is rare in nature.

Now that I think about it, it looked like one of those Egyptian temples with the giant columns. But, given that, at the time, I was more Christian than Egyptian, I called the place "the cathedral."
I brought a few friends from the group there.

We also went all the way to Big Sur once, to see the ocean.

Berkeley wasn't far from our seminar. I asked for permission to pay Landis a visit, and my old jalopy made it there without a hitch. It took me an hour.

I found Landis at the student center. He was really happy to see me. His friends wanted to know what I was doing among the redwoods, and when I told them, they thought the whole thing was ridiculous.

We went to the house Landis was staying in. It was on campus and had a small attached garage. We talked all afternoon on the roof of that garage, lying in the sun on an old mattress, as if we were at the beach.

In the evening I returned to my redwoods. I have to say, after all that thinking, I was starting to ask myself some serious questions about what I was doing.

One morning I got a letter from Gerhart and Vera which, surprisingly, was postmarked from Pasadena. The last letter, they'd sent from Germany.

Since then, they'd eventually seen that Gerhart wouldn't find work in Germany as a musician. At the invitation of Vera's family, they traveled to Boston.

Her family wanted Gerhart to make ends meet American-style, meaning, play in fancy nightclubs. Why not? But he said:

No way. That's not my style. I'm a classical pianist, and that's it.

He was really depressed, and so was Vera. The family sent them to a psychiatrist. The psychiatrist then told the family:

It's very simple. Leave them alone. Give them $400, a plane ticket for wherever they want to go, and say good-bye.

Gerhart and Vera asked themselves: "Where should we go? We could try Pasadena. That's where Alan lives." They arrived in the L.A. airport and went straight to my house, but I wasn't home. My father said that I was up north, among the redwoods, and explained what I was doing.

And so they wrote me.

The letter began with news, but the second part took a different tone.
Gerhart said straight out: "Alan, you're making a mistake."
He tried to talk me out of the path I'd chosen—he was very anti-Christian.
It wasn't that he was against Jesus, he just didn't believe Jesus was the son of God.
And anyway, he didn't think it was the right way to understand and practice a religion.

His arguments echoed my talks with Landis and added to the doubts I'd been having.
I answered him. He sent me several letters over the next few weeks.

I woke up one morning and found that I had become a heretic.

That same day, in the middle of a meeting attended by all 30 of us, I stood up and said:

I don't agree with this anymore.
I think all of it is wrong. This isn't the right way to look at life, or spirituality.
I'm going.

I said good-bye, gathered up my things, got my car, and left.

240

32

Gerhart and Vera had settled in Pasadena. He was playing the organ in various churches to make a living, but it went against his convictions and he didn't understand a thing about the American liturgy.

Vera delivered milk.

Meanwhile, Patzi had decided that I wasn't capable of loving her and had broken off our engagement. She was right. She soon met another man.

None of that gave rise to any hard feelings, by the way. I took part in Egypt's wedding like a member of the family. I was even at the wedding rehearsal. In those days there was a full dress rehearsal before the actual wedding.

I didn't return to my studies at Redlands. I realized that what I wanted was Europe. I didn't like America any more.
Sure, I liked the country, the landscape, the people—but I no longer liked the mentality.
Even though there's a lot that's good about the American mentality, it somehow doesn't plumb the depths of existence.
And that's why, in some ways, America is not doing well.
Most Americans live on the surface of existence; I wanted to know its depths.
I don't know if that means anything to you, but it's what I sincerely believed.

My plan from then on was to save up enough
money to go to France.

Why France?

I haven't talked about it, because it relates to my
adult life, and we're not going to say much about
that, but I do have to tell you, just to make things
clear, that when I arrived in Normandy in '45,
I met a young Frenchwoman. On April 1st, to be
exact. April Fool's Day. She was wearing a little
raincoat. She was adorable. When I was in Bad
Wiessee, I saw her again while on leave in Paris.
After my breakup with Patzi, I wrote her a few
letters, which Gerhart translated. He also
translated her answers, because at the time
I didn't speak a word of French, and she spoke
no English.

Anyway, we agreed that I would go join her and
that we'd start a new life in France.

I got a job at a local hospital in Pasadena. At the time it was fairly easy to get a job as an orderly. A nurse gave me a quick overview of the various things I'd be doing.

The male and female patients were separated, so with rare exceptions, I dealt only with men. It was very interesting work, by the way.

I learned how to give patients catheters and sponge baths. Back then they kept post-operative patients in bed for a while. Nowadays they're pretty much chucked out as quickly as possible.

I took care of some very sick people, and I saw a lot of them die. If I was working nights, I'd often transport bodies to the basement morgue, and put them in a refrigerated drawer. The bodies had to be prepared so that they wouldn't "leak," and so on.

At night, when it was quiet, our team would clean thousands of needles, because in those days we'd collect the used ones and sharpen them, and then, like a lot of other things, they'd go in the autoclave.

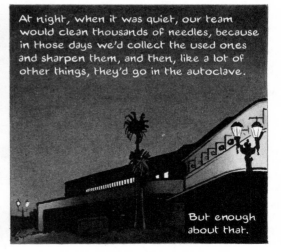

But enough about that.

Gerhart and Vera were renting a small house. There was a piano in the front room, so Gerhart could compose. Vera had become head of the milk delivery team, and it was her job to keep morale up. It was a strange situation for people who had kept company with Thomas Mann, Paul Klee, Ezra Pound, and Jean Cocteau.

Gerhart met an expressionist dancer in Hollywood. They put on a show in a tiny little theater. I saw it; it was very good.

After the show, he went to the back office to collect his money.
The office was empty. The owners had taken off with the cash.

When he found them, they said frankly:

We do that all the time.

Gerhart started laughing. He said:

That's not right.

There was nothing he could do.

244

Many of the artists that Gerhart had known in Europe had fled to California during the war and become successful. My dad would lend us his car, and Gerhart and I would go visit them in Beverly Hills or Hollywood.

I remember a very old lady, I don't know her name, who had a Salvador Dali portrait of her hanging in her front hall.

I also remember a couple who lived in an amazing villa in the Hollywood hills, near Griffith Observatory, James Dean's famous planetarium. You entered from the top, because the house was built on a very steep slope. There were two-story floor-to-ceiling windows looking out on all of Los Angeles. Smog had only just begun to show up then, nothing too bad yet. Forty miles of lights right at our feet; now that was impressive.
I was seeing these ultra-luxurious, modern places with my eyes still full of images of wartime Europe, and it unsettled me.

Another couple was renting a house in the wilderness, right by the Sierra Nevada foothills, in the middle of an oak forest. One evening we went there for dinner.

The house was beautiful. It was in the middle of nowhere, just forest and mountains, with a lawn in the front.

In those days, Californian houses could have vast plots of land.

We ate outside, on a large terrace. Each person sat in a leather-covered armchair, the kind you'd find in a French medieval castle. The chair backs rose higher than our heads.

Our host said:

At nightfall you're going to see something amazing. I won't tell you what it is; it's a surprise.

We finished eating—dessert and everything. It was dusk now.

Okay. It's time.

Three or four little foxes came down from the mountain.

They played on the lawn, just like kids.

When they'd finished playing, they drew closer and came up onto the terrace.

Don't say anything. Don't even breathe. Keep quiet.

The little foxes circled us, behind our chairs. They wanted the food, you see.

Then they jumped up onto those tall chair backs and kept circling the table—foxes have an incredible sense of balance—by leaping from chair to chair.

Can you picture it? Unbelievable. They were testing us.

When they saw that all was well, they jumped down and ate our leftovers.

We sat there for a solid hour, completely still, while all this was going on. And then they left.

It's the same thing every night, except they can't go all around the table if there aren't enough people.

If it's just the two of us, they hop from one chair to the other until they get up the courage to jump down.

They're not tame. It's just that no human has ever hurt them.

You don't have to believe me, but I swear, that's exactly how it happened.

248

33

One time, we went on an important trip.
I talked to you before about the coastal redwoods.
Well, they aren't the largest ones in California.
The oldest and most massive are in the Sierra Nevada.
Gerhart and Vera wanted to see them. I'm glad they did.
They knew how to appreciate things of real value.
Gerhart said he'd cover gas and all other traveling costs.
No small thing, seeing as he was completely broke.
He persuaded my dad to lend us his car for a few days.
We set off.

They wanted to drive through the desert,
but it wasn't the most impressive part.
We'd have done better to take the
coastal road; it would've been prettier.

I remember a little Mexican restaurant
on the side of the road, nice and clean,
that served very spicy food.
For the first time I understood the benefits
of eating spicy food in countries with
swelteringly hot weather.

When you sweat normally, in that kind of
heat, you hardly notice you're sweating
because it evaporates right away. But after
that meal, our faces and bodies were
covered with a light, even film of sweat
that lingered for a while.

It made the slightest breeze refreshing.

Later we drove through farming areas, where huge fields stretched out into the distance. Finally, we arrived at the base of the mountain, where Sequoia Park is.

Taking that route is a startling experience. As we climbed higher and higher, we wondered, "Where are those big trees?"

All of a sudden, we took a turn and saw a tree, far away, jutting out of the side of the mountain—but what a tree! Given the distance and the forest surrounding it, it looked enormous.

Unbelievable tree trunks began to appear on both sides of the car. We were in awe. . .

I stopped at a tourist office. They rented out cabins for the night, which was perfect for us, since we couldn't afford a hotel.

Our accommodations were very basic, a log cabin with seven rooms all in a row and a small kitchen where you could put a camping stove (though we didn't have one). There were boards for beds, with dirty straw pallets for mattresses. We'd brought our own blankets.

We bought some food from a small grocery store—cold, plain, and quick. We were in a hurry to go deep into the forest.

We set out on a footpath. I was surprised to see so few people. A man on his own, every now and again. A couple. Hardly anyone at all.

We realized we were being followed by does.

They came very close. Fawns trotted alongside them. The eyes of does, when they're not afraid, are absolutely extraordinary. It was as if we were some other kind of harmless animal.

There were signs that read:

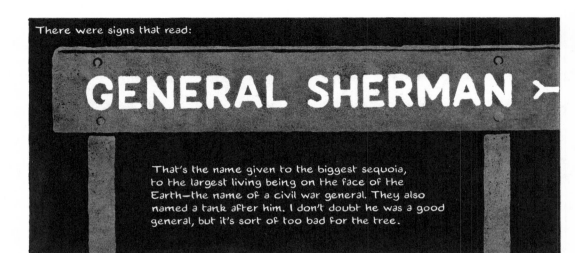

GENERAL SHERMAN ⌐

That's the name given to the biggest sequoia, to the largest living being on the face of the Earth—the name of a civil war general. They also named a tank after him. I don't doubt he was a good general, but it's sort of too bad for the tree.

I'd read about that tree before I saw it. At the time it was nearly 250 feet tall.
It has probably kept on growing, since it's still alive.
It was about 35 feet in diameter and 85 feet around, and it was thought to be 5,000 years old. Since then I hear they've halfed his age.
Lucky tree.

We passed all sorts of giants while waiting to catch sight of it. The undergrowth was much sparser and drier than in the coastal forest.

All of a sudden it was right in front of us.

You know, you can't
begin to imagine
that tree until you've
seen it, and you can't quite
grasp it when you do.
You just feel it, that's all.
Besides, you can't really
see it.
If you step back,
it blends into the forest.
If you look up,
the top gets lost
in a tangle of branches.
All you can see is its
trunk—its immense,
awe-inspiring trunk,
with its thick, red,
rough bark.

Conversation with a Giant Sequoia Redwood

Journey, swooping up from a white heat-frozen desert.
Mountain heights tempered in pure blue respiration,
Aflame throughout four rust-red centuries.
Sequoia is an Indian name.

The legend, where is it?
Who has seen you?
The fawn
The snake
Fires
Count back to The Tree
Where your time begins,
Double that
And my mother tossed a pinion
Whirling in the air —
I have no legends!

I am the last of a long line of arrows
That strayed from Apollo
Or a post that held up the earth
While Jehovah was painting it
Or the mast of a sailing moon
Stranded on a voyage from Mars.

Do not look at me too long — it is dangerous.
(Why have I disturbed this peace?)
Go back to your city
Your legends
And Time!

California, 1948

After that, we followed a long trail.
A very narrow trail. There wasn't a soul around.

At the end of the path we had to go around a large boulder.

The ground was nothing but stones; an iron guardrail ran along the edge.

When she reached the bar, Vera let out a horrific scream.

She turned around and darted back toward the rock.

The guardrail overlooked a sheer drop of a thousand feet (according to the sign).

Vera, trembling, huddled behind the rock, clutching it.

There's no way. I can't look at that.

We'll head back, then.

Absolutely not! Go on!

I'll stay here, where it's safe. I'll be fine, I won't get bored. I'll do some thinking.

It's true, she'll be fine staying here. She can do it.

We left Vera behind her rock and again set out on the trail—if you can call it that. It was getting dangerous.

I didn't know that Gerhart had an excellent sense of balance, but it soon became clear. He was 20 years older than me, and could seem frail, but he certainly wasn't. If he gave you a good, firm handshake, his strong pianist's hand could easily crush yours.

We came to a very difficult passage, a sort of gravel waterfall, on a steep slope. One wrong move and you'd tumble to the bottom, nothing to break your fall.

There was a narrow track, made by animals—barely a foot wide.

Take tiny steps. Don't try to put one foot in front of the other. Put one foot forward and scoot the other up behind it. And don't look at anything other than where you're putting your feet.

Okay.

I'd learned that in the Alps.

After what seemed like a long time the trail reappeared. Still dangerous, but not as bad.

Finally we arrived at a lovely little turquoise lake.

We absolutely have to take a swim.

I don't know. I bet the water's freezing.

I can't imagine finding such a beautiful lake and not becoming one with it. Stay there if you want, but I'm going for a swim.

All right, me too.

We stripped down, but kept our underwear—which was kind of dumb, really, since it would stay wet, but Gerhart was a bit of a prude.

We swam back and forth across the lake. It wasn't very deep, and the water was ice cold.

After that we headed back. The exertion dried us off.

We met up with Vera, who liked the story of the little lake. We returned to camp.

I've said that Gerhart wasn't handsome. His nose was crooked; I never asked him how it had gotten pushed over to the right side. Maybe he was born like that. I should have asked him; it was silly of me not to.
When I was young, I was silly about a lot of things.

Vera wasn't beautiful, either, but to me she was, just like other women in my life were beautiful to me—my Cope grandmother, Martha, and a few others who I knew weren't pretty.
Vera had a beauty that appealed to me and certainly came from the soul, however you want to define that word. It's something much deeper than character or blood, and it makes a person radiant.
There are some attractive people whose beauty doesn't strike you, or strikes you only in a very superficial way.

The next morning we were woken up in the wee hours by noise outside.

Several garbage cans sat in the alleyway beside our cabin, and we discovered bears rifling through them with their muzzles and paws.

The tourist office people had warned us about this, saying that we could go outside very quietly, without getting close to the animals. They wouldn't bother us if we left them alone. So we went out, giving them a wide berth.

It was really interesting to see them at work.

Later, at daybreak, people started making noise, and the bears left.

So, in a nutshell, that was our sequoias trip. The ride home was long, hot, and tiring. There wasn't much to do but drive.

34

Before I talk about leaving the States, I'd like to mention Benner, a friend of Egypt's and mine.

Ben was the shy, secretive type, a smart guy who'd never managed to graduate high school. He was, in fact, discovering his homosexuality. He'd never had sex or anything, but he knew he was gay and was distraught.

I spent a lot of time with him then. Although he was a solitary guy, he got along well with me. He was crazy about films and actors, so he'd often suggest going to the movies in Hollywood.

We'd borrow his parents' car, and I'd drive.

One evening he asked me to kiss him, just to see what it felt like. I said no.

That ended our friendship.
To this day,
I still regret it.

When I caught up with Egypt many years later—almost 30 years later—I wrote to her: "I've tried to get in touch with Ben, but haven't heard anything. Can you tell me what he's up to?" She wrote back simply: "Don't try contacting him, it's pointless. Let's not talk about it; I can't talk about it." But I insisted, and, finally, it was Egypt's husband who answered me by adding a few lines to the bottom of a letter: "Ben has been dead for a long time now."

Ben died at the age of 37 in Mexico City.
He was the head of the Mexican operations of a big American cosmetics company.
Apparently he'd started drinking heavily and died of a cerebral embolism.

And there's no way of knowing whether a simple gesture might have changed his destiny.

35

Finally I managed to save up enough money to buy a ticket on the steamship "United States."
Gerhart wrote me a few letters of introduction to his friends in France, particularly Fernand Crommelynck.
I said good-bye to everyone and left.

In New York the dockers were on strike.
I was stranded there with little money, a huge trunk, and some luggage.

I called Lou.

The strike lasted a month. Lou put me up. He was living with his in-laws and pregnant wife. I remember her making her own ravioli on the kitchen table.

One day I was finally able to board that huge ocean liner.

I was in third class, of course.
And by third class, I mean really third class.

I met an Englishwoman on board who'd just broken off her engagement to an American and was returning to England. It hadn't worked out, partly because of the guy, but mostly because of his family.

She was very nice and quite eccentric. We ate our meals together; they were included in the ticket price.

On the second day, she said to me:

Alan, won't you buy me a beer or something? Are you totally broke?

You know, I've got some dollars left over, and it's not as though I'll be using them at home. I'll give them to you. Just tell your parents to send me some stuff I can't get in England.

I was broke all right. I could offer her only cigarettes; I had a carton of them.

She wrote out a list for me that I later sent to Caroline, my stepmother, who wondered what kind of woman I'd met. Among the things she wanted were purple lingerie and green stockings. I never forgot that.

The different classes were kept on different decks, totally cut off from one another. It was out of the question for a third-class passenger to wander into first class, or even second. There was a whole system of private elevators.

First-class passengers had top-notch entertainment every night; in second class they had dances; in third, nothing whatsoever. But the Englishwoman wanted to dance.

In a fairly quiet, secluded area of our deck, we found a small ladder that hooked onto the ship's rail.

In the evenings we'd get dressed up as best we could. I had my one good suit and she had a nice dress. We'd set up the ladder and risk our necks climbing from one deck to another, with the sea below us. The weather was calm.

And then we'd go dancing.

One time they played that game where the music stops suddenly and you have to stay frozen in position, you know? We did that really well, and one by one the other dancers were eliminated and disappeared around us.

When there were only three couples left, I said to her:

What should we do? We might win if we keep this up!

Oh well, we'll see.

And we did win! The prize was a bottle of champagne. It was very welcome, because during those nights I couldn't afford to drink, or could have maybe one beer, nothing more.

We drank our champagne and snuck back the way we'd come. But we never had the nerve to go up there again.

36

I arrived in France and went to Paris to live with my future wife's family.

Thanks to a grant, I was able to take a French-language course. I got around on a second-hand bike.

I kept it for 45 years, up until two summers ago, when it was stolen.

When I started being able to speak French, I registered at the École des Métiers d'Art, rue de Thorigny, in the Marais—where the Picasso Museum is now.

I wanted to learn pottery. I'd been thinking about it since before the war and had started working with clay in America. I liked it. I wanted to do it for a living.

It was a good school, and it was there that I made a real friend, Pierre Lèbe, a guy from the Lot region, in the Southwest. He was very talented.

I decided that it was time to go see Gerhart's friend, Crommelynck. He lived in la Patte d'Oie d'Herblay, northwest of Paris. Not exactly next door when you're on a bike.

I called him up and he invited me to lunch. He'd already received a letter from Gerhart telling him about me. I looked for my letter of recommendation anyway, but, to my great surprise, I was unable to find it, even though I had kept it carefully tucked away in my things.

When the day came, I set out wearing a pair of Bavarian lederhosen. It was summertime.

Crommelynck welcomed me warmly. He lived with his first wife—they'd separated, but had gotten back together again. I gabbled on in my broken French.
I'm sure he found me a little strange; I had a bit of a devil-may-care attitude at the time.

Later, my fiancée admitted that she'd found Gerhart's letter, read it, and burned it, because Gerhart had asked Crommelynck to talk me out of marrying her.

I resented Gerhart. He wrote to me a little later to say that he and Vera couldn't make a living in Pasadena and had sought refuge with Henry Miller at his house in Big Sur. Gerhart had known Miller since before the war, in Paris.

Later, in '53, I wanted to break my silence. I was living in France's Berri region at the time. I didn't know how to get in touch with Gerhart, and while I didn't expect him to be in Big Sur anymore, I wrote to Miller to ask how to reach him.

In response, Miller sent me one of those penny postcards, where you write the address on one side, the message on the other, and drop it in the mailbox. He wasn't very wealthy at the time. He believed Gerhart and Vera were in Mexico. Where exactly, he had no idea. He suggested I read "Plexus," which had just come out.

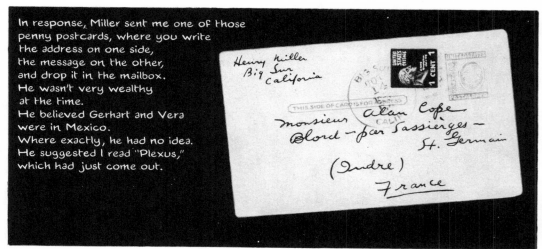

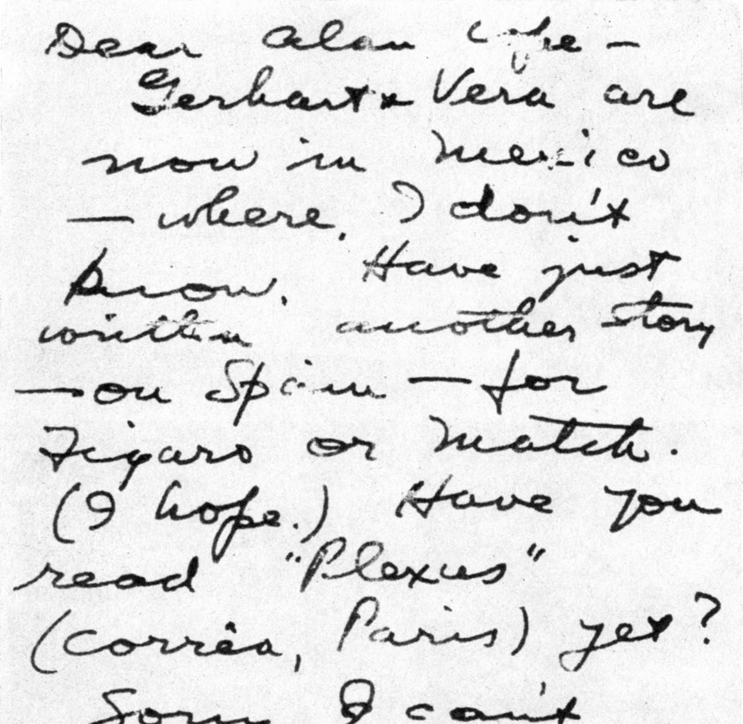
Dear Alan Cohe—
Gerhart & Vera are
now in Mexico
— where, I don't
know. Have just
written another story
— on Spain — for
Figaro or Match.
(I hope.) Have you
read "Plexus"
(Corrêa, Paris) yet?
Sorry I can't
write more. Back
2 months now.
Had a marvelous
7 months abroad
& will return
next year, I
trust. Henry Miller

In the end it was Gerhart who contacted me.
They were living in a town called Guanajuato, where Gerhart taught at the conservatory.
He found Mexico poorer but more humane than America. Artists were treated better, with more respect. And most of all, he felt he could help people.
He composed, while Vera published her poems, translated into Spanish.

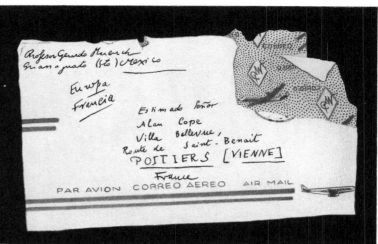

We corresponded until my divorce, in 1958.
I was terribly unhappy, and I again got it into my head that Gerhart had poisoned my marriage. I wrote him to say I was cutting him out of my life. I was wrong, of course, but in my state...

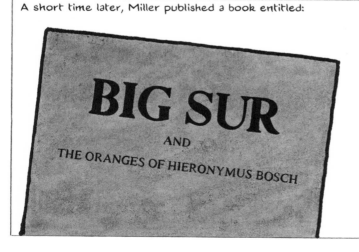

I got one last letter from him. I barely opened it, but didn't throw it away, either.
After that, nothing.

A short time later, Miller published a book entitled:

BIG SUR

AND

THE ORANGES OF HIERONYMUS BOSCH

A great book, I might add. Miller, as he always did, talks about his life in Big Sur and the people he met there. Several passages were devoted to Gerhart.

Here they are. Perhaps you'd like to read them.

It was also at Anderson Creek that Gerhart Muench used to practice—on an old upright that Emil White had borrowed from someone. Now and then Gerhart gave us a concert, on this same "distempered" clavichord. Motorists would occasionally pull up short in front of Emil's cabin to listen to Gerhart practice. When Gerhart was broke and discouraged, often in a suicidal mood, I would urge him (seriously) to move the piano out, put it alongside the road, and do his stuff. I had a notion that if he would do it often enough some impresario would happen along and offer him a concert tour. (Gerhart is known all over Europe for his piano concerts.) But Gerhart never fell for the idea. Certainly it would have been vulgar and showy, but Americans dote on that sort of thing. Think of the publicity he might have had, had some enterprising soul discovered him sitting by the roadside hammering his way through Scriabin's ten sonatas!

(...)

Now and then, often in the middle of a problem, I wonder if the fellow who was here the day before riffling through my water colors, I wonder if when he paused to look twice at a certain "monstrosity" he had the faintest notion of the circumstances in which it was conceived and executed? Would he believe me, I wonder, if I told him that it was done one-two-three, just like that, and five more to boot, while Gerhart Muench was practicing on my broken-down piano? Would he have the least inkling that it was Ravel who inspired it? Ravel of Gaspard de la nuit? It was while Gerhart was going over and over the "Scarbo" that I suddenly lost all control of myself and began to paint music. It was like a thousand tractors going up and down my spine at high speed, the way Gerhart's playing affected me. The faster the rhythm, the more thunderous and ominous the music, the better my brushes flew over the paper. I had no time to pause or reflect. On! On! Good Garbo! Sweet Garbo! Good Launcelot Garbo, Scarbo, Barbo! Faster! Faster! Faster! The paper was dripping paint on all sides. I was dripping with perspiration. I wanted to scratch my ass, but there was no time for it. On with it, Scarbo! *Dance*, you gazebo! Gerhart's arms are moving like flails. Mine too. If he goes pianissimo, and he can go pianissimo just as beautifully as he can fortissimo, I go pianissimo too. Which means I spray the trees with insecticide, cross my *t*'s and dot my *i*'s. I don't know where I am or what I'm doing. Does it matter? In one hand I have two brushes, in the other three, all of them saturated with pigment. So it goes, from one painting to another, and all the while singing, dancing, rocking, weaving, tottering, mumbling, cursing, shouting. Just for good measure I slide one of them to the floor and grind my heels into it. (Slavic ecstasy.) By the time Gerhart has sandpapered his finger tips I've turned out a half-dozen water colors (complete with coda, cadenza and vermiform appendix) that would scare the daylight out of a buzzard, octaroon or tomtit.

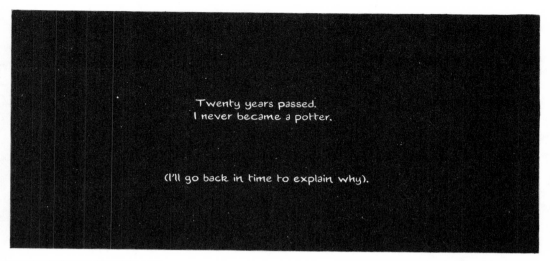

37

Twenty years passed.
I never became a potter.

(I'll go back in time to explain why).

In 1950, because of a mistake by the grants committee, my funds were cut off three months short of my graduation from the Métiers d'Art. I was already married and the father of my first son.

I had to find a job right away.

I took a trip to Caen to apply for a job as a worker in a brick factory.

I remember arriving at dawn and going into a small café for a cup of coffee at the counter.

What do you want in it?

Nothing, just coffee.

She served me my coffee in a wine glass.

How much is that?

How much is a coffee without calva?

She didn't know the price of coffee without Calvados liqueur.

I then met the factory owner, who described the job. It was hard work with little pay.

He showed me the workers' quarters— a depressing-looking row of shabby brick houses. The only modern convenience was running water.

We might have been willing to rough it for a while had the money been decent, but it was too depressing and the chance of advancement was nil. I said no and returned to Paris.

Luckily, America, which had gotten me into that mess by canceling my grant, saved my hide. American military bases were hiring translator-interpreters in Poitiers. My French was middling, but I didn't have a choice; I had to give it a shot.

I got on the train wearing my best clothes: a fairly elegant and newish-looking leather jacket, a decent pair of pants, and a pair of high boots.
I'd reinforced them by gluing new soles onto the old ones; a lot of people did that back then.

When I got to Poitiers, I went to the office of Mr. Henry Miglio.

274

I was shown into an enormous room lined with at least ten desks. Behind each one sat a translator hard at work, with Mr. Miglio overseeing them from the other end of the room.

I walked forward several feet, trying to appear self-confident and make a good first impression.

All of a sudden I had the distinct feeling that one of my soles had come unglued and fallen off. So I looked over my shoulder and saw it lying on the ground behind me.

Without even thinking, I swiveled around and stood in front of my sole, with Mr. Miglio's eyes on me. I stepped on it firmly to reattach it to my boot. It worked.

I passed the test. I made a few major mistakes, but I was hired anyway.

Don't worry about your mistakes. With some practice you'll be a good translator. I have to say, I was impressed by the way you kept your cool when your sole fell off.

It was that little test that determined my entire professional life. I went back into the army as a civilian employee and left it only when I retired.

What was my job? I did the work of a lawyer without being one—which is why money was always tight. I handled disputes between the local population and soldiers on military bases. Things that could range from running a red light to murder.

Basically, I filled out tons of paperwork, but also did some interesting things. I interpreted during trials and was good at it—I helped out a lot of young people in prison. Some of them still write me today.

When the American bases in France closed down, I left, with my second wife, for Worms, Germany, where we stayed until I retired.

For 18 months, while waiting for my wife to retire, I drove a small valuables delivery van, with a locked safe in the back, along the roads of the Palatinate. I was 50 years old.

I'd take the 6:20 a.m. train from Worms and would read a German newspaper in the meantime. That helped me improve my German without ever really studying it.

I'd get to the Wiesbaden station at 7:25 and from there would walk to work. By 8 o'clock, I sat behind the wheel of my van.

I'd make the rounds of the dozen or so military stores scattered throughout the Palatinate. Some were in town, others out in the country. The most isolated ones were, of course, the most secret.

I transported official mail, packages, and specific items ordered by the stores. I dropped them off, and they'd give me another batch to be brought back to headquarters.

Every day, in person, the store supervisors would drop the accumulated money into a slot on the top of the safe. Sometimes I'd have huge sums of money. Right after the servicemen's payday, there might be over $100,000.

I was alone and unarmed. Maybe people knew, but I was never attacked.

I was always afraid of the car being stolen. One time it broke down, and I had to leave it on the side of the road. Luckily I didn't have to go too far to get help.

I'd picnic in the countryside. It was bucolic and cheap, and I didn't have to let my cargo out of sight.
One day, as I was eating my sandwiches, I saw a bunch of rabbits.

As I watched, they arranged themselves in a large circle, all facing inward, like the knights of the Round Table.

Time passed. They held their quiet little ceremony, without moving an inch, and then they disappeared. Strange, isn't it?

One of the stores, the most remote one, was out in the middle of nowhere, in the forest, up on a hill. An armed guard watched over the facility's entrance day and night. Obviously the place had something to do with secret weapons.

Whenever I arrived, the same guard was pretty much always there, a young black man. He was really intimidating—very tough-looking, and handsome, too.

At first he didn't like me; he thought I was the enemy. But then, he probably thought everyone was. I had a devil of a time persuading him to let me park where I wanted. He scared me.

Bit by bit he realized I wasn't the enemy, and we finally became quite friendly. He'd be happy to see me, and we'd exchange some pleasantries.
That guy must have suffered a great deal at the hands of whites, that's for sure.

On a less serious note, let me tell you a little story. One day I was leaving that place, and I had to take a steep slope leading out of the facility's tucked-away forest and onto a fairly busy road.

It was the middle of summer and very hot. I was wearing sandals. When I reached the bottom of the hill, I began to downshift and I hit the brake.

An excruciating pain shot through my right foot. Unbearable!

OW!

But I had to keep my foot on the brake. I was coming up on the road at a right angle, and I could see the cars driving by.

Finally, still screaming, I managed to come to a stop.

I couldn't begin to imagine what was happening to me. It felt like I'd been shot in the foot. When I took my shoe off, I saw several bees squashed between my foot and the insole.

My boss was fairly pleased with me.
If I finished early, I was supposed to
return to headquarters to help out
with the office work.
That didn't thrill me, so most of the
time I'd cheat and get out of it.
There was a library in the last military
facility I visited.
I'd go and take out books.

I'd park on a corner and
read at the steering wheel
until 5 p.m. That's how
I became familiar with
Rimbaud, in an English
translation.

Then I'd go drop off the
van and take the train
back to Worms.

All things considered,
that was a pretty boring
and tedious time.
I thought to myself, okay,
here's what I'm going to do.
I'm not happy at all, neither
with myself nor my life.
Since I have free time
every day, I'm going to
think on my past and
make some sense out of it.
Because I've had
a strange life.

I tried hard to see my existence from the very beginning,
and, as you know, my recollections go back to my very
early childhood.
I tried to look at everything clearly, for the most part in
chronological order. I tried to recall people, situations, and
words. The good things I'd done, and the bad. The ways in
which others had—consciously and unconsciously—shaped
me. I did that day after day for 18 months.

You don't make that kind of trip in one day.

The experiment soon became very interesting.
I won't go into details about what I learned,
but let's just say it was a lot.
That was the beginning of my life
as a philosopher—if I dare call myself
one—because it taught me to think.
I broadened my scope to civilization,
politics, religion.
I took advantage of the little library
I'd borrowed that Rimbaud from,
and did some research.
I didn't write anything,
but it did me a lot of good.

After 18 months, I came to the conclusion that I hadn't lived my own life. I hadn't lived the life of MYSELF. I had lived the life of the person others had wanted me to be; that's different.

And that person had
never existed.

We came back to France to retire,
my wife and I. Among the things
I'd realized in the Palatinate was my
love for Gerhart and Vera and the great
wrong I'd done them.
I was overcome by the desire to tell them
so, and to ask for their forgiveness.
Gerhart had been overbearing,
but in the end he'd been right.

How could I find them?

First I sent off some "shot in the dark" cards.
Nothing. Two years went by.
In 1978, while going through my things, I found Gerhart's last letter,
which I'd received exactly 20 years earlier—the one I'd opened,
to see if it contained anything earthshaking,
but had never really read.

At the end of the letter,
I noticed two lines:
"Try to get your hands
on the translated works of
Octavio Paz. He told me
he was beginning to be
appreciated in France."
The name was familiar.
I soon learned that Paz
was both a diplomat
and an internationally
renowned poet.
I wrote to the Editions
Gallimard publishing house.
I wrote to Casa Velázquez,
in Madrid, because I thought
I'd heard that Paz had
written a preface there
in 1971.
I wrote to the Mexican
embassy in Paris, and,
finally, their cultural
department sent me
his address in Mexico.
I wrote to Octavio Paz,
asking: "Do you know the
address of Gerhart and
Vera Muench?"

And Paz responded:

Le 10 avril, 1979.

Monsieur Alan Cope
3, Rue Suzanne-Cothonneau
F - 17410 Saint-Martin-de-Ré
France.

Monsieur,

J'ai pu retrouver, grace à
Madame Michèle Alban, l'adresse de vos
amis, le musicien Gerhard Muench et sa
femme Vera:

Gerhard et Vera Muench
Calle Morelos 166
Tacámbaro, Michoacán
México.

Cordialmente,

Octavio Paz

P.s. La boîte postale de Gérard Muench:
Apartado Postal 25, Tacámbaro, Mich.

Lerma 143-601. México 5. D. F.

"Sir,
I was able, with the help of Mrs. Michèle Alban, to find the address
of your friends Gerhart Muench, the musician, and his wife, Vera:
Gerhart and Vera Muench
Calle Morelos 166
Tacámbaro, Michoacán
México.
Cordially,
Octavio Paz
P.S. Gérard Muench's post office box is:
    Apartado Postal 25, Tacámbaro, Mich."

38

So that's how I found Gerhart and Vera.
I sent them a letter, and I got one back.
Both were over 70.
They had arrived in Mexico in 1953 and had never left.
Gerhart had taught at the Mexico National Conservatory and at Mexico University.
He had composed a lot and played a lot.
Vera sent me a bilingual edition of her poems.

ESTACIONES

VERA MUENCH

They had both been semiretired since 1972, living in the small colonial town of Tacámbaro, in Michoacán province. They lived in a 19th-century house, with every room opening onto a patio filled with shrubs, flowers, and birds.
They were still active, but old age was beginning to affect them.
They lived in isolation. Gerhart had a bad eye that was getting worse.
His fingers were stiffening up.

I had sent them some pictures of myself.
In return I received a Mexican magazine featuring a lengthy article illustrated
by this double portrait.
To recreate the way they looked when I knew them, when they were so much younger,
you'd have to erase the years from their faces.
Perhaps a drawing could do that.

I had continued my process of reflection since my time in the Palatinate, and I had grown a lot.
I'd become more and more opposed to the civilization I lived in, despite being quite fond of many of its aspects.
At the same time, I'd realized I was messing up my existence and that the human race was messing its own up too—and for pretty much the same reasons: failing to make the most of intelligence and creativity; overcrowding by too many dogmas, false values, and wrong thinking; a kind of psychic illness that afflicts the human race and prevents people from knowing what to do with their lives; disastrous habits; an appalling waste of the earth's resources. An inability, caused by self-obsession, to open up to the true spirituality of existence.
I felt myself becoming extreme and intransigent on all these issues.
I wrote to Gerhart:
"I am totally against everyone else's opinions, and everyone else is against mine. It's unbelievable, BUT I'M WAKING UP!"

He was thrilled to hear that, and from that day on we had a voluminous correspondence. He told me I was the only person he had left, and I think I helped ease the bitterness of the end of his life.
Despite his bad eye, which was getting worse and worse, he'd copy out for me, by hand, page after page of books from his library, things he thought were important, to try to take me to a place I'd never been before.
Page after page of Bachelard, of Henri Bosco, of Frédéric Mistral, especially the "Poem of the Rhône," which he could read in Provençal. He had me read the tales of Hoffman, whom he called "the most imaginative fantasist of all time." And Hölderlin, "that supreme and divine oracular poet."
Whenever I could, I tried to listen to works by Messiaen, Boulez, and Stockhausen, which he'd first introduced into Mexico.

And that's how, after forming an embryonic conscience for myself, all alone in my van, through finding Gerhart once again, at the age of 55, I was born.

Having lost his sight in one eye, he'd send me this kind of thing—here, excerpts from the works of Bachelard, a French philosopher, interspersed with his own comments.

BACHELARD.   Réponse s'il te plaît!!

Poétique du Rêve, page 161. Mais l'être du monde, rêve-t-il? Ah, jadis, avant la "culture", qui en aurait douté? Chacun sait que le métal, dans la mine, lentement mûrissait. Et comment mûrir sans rêver? Et la terre — quand elle ne tournait pas — comment, sans rêves, eût-elle mûri ses saisons? Les grands rêves de cosmicité sont garants de l'immobilité de la Terre. Que la raison, après de longs travaux, vienne prouver que la Terre tourne, il n'en reste pas moins qu'une telle déclaration est oniriquement absurde. Qui pourrait convaincre un rêveur de cosmos que la terre vire-volte sur elle-même? et qu'elle vole dans le ciel? On ne rêve pas avec des idées enseignées.

Poétique de l'Espace: On lit les pages de Bosco comme un emboîtement des réserves de force dans les châteaux intérieurs du courage.
En relisant Malicroix j'entends sur le Toit de la Redousse passer, le sabot de fer du songe.
On ne voit jamais l'image en première instance. Toute grande image a un fond onirique insondable et c'est sur ce fond onirique que le passé personnel met des couleurs particulières. Dans le règne de l'imagination absolue, on est jeune très tard. Il faut perdre le paradis terrestre pour y vraiment vivre dans la sublimation absolue qui transcende toute passion.
La poésie nous donne non pas tant la nostalgie de la jeunesse, ce qui serait vulgaire, mais la nostalgie des expressions de la jeunesse. Ou remonte de la primitivité.
— Toute âme profonde a son au-delà personnel. —
Les mots sont des petites maisons, avec cave et grenier. Le sens commun séjourne au rez-de-chaussée, toujours prêt au "commerce extérieur", de plein pied avec autrui, ce passant qui n'est jamais un rêveur. Monter l'escalier de la maison du mot, c'est, de degré en degré, abstraire. Descendre à la cave, c'est rêver, c'est se perdre dans les lointains contours d'une mythologie incertaine, c'est chercher dans les mots des trésors introuvables. Monter et descendre, dans le mot même

c'est la vie du poète. Monter trop haut, descendre trop bas est permis au poète qui joint le terrestre à l'aérien. Seul le philosophe serait-il condamné parf ses pairs à vivre toujours au rez-de-chaussée ?

—

Flamme d'une chandelle (p 58)

La flamme est une verticalité habitée. Tout rêveur de flamme sait que la flamme est vivante. Elle garantit sa verticalité par de sensibles réflexes. Qu'un incident de combustion vienne troubler l'élan zénithal, aussitôt la flamme réagit. Un rêveur de volonté verticalisante qui prend sa leçon devant la flamme apprend qu'il doit se redresser. Il retrouve la volonté de brûler haut, d'aller de toutes ses forces au sommet de l'ardeur.—

La flamme est un sablier qui coule vers le haut. Flamme et sablier, dans la méditation paisible, expriment la communion du temps léger et du temps lourd. J'aimerais rêver au temps, à la durée qui s'écoule et à la durée qui s'envole si je pouvais réunir en ma cellule imaginaire la chandelle et le sablier.

—

Les rêveries de la petite lumière nous ramèneront au réduit de la familiarité. Il semble qu'il y ait en nous des coins sombres qui ne tolèrent qu'une lumière vacillante...

—

P. de l'Espace. pag 40 sur l'Antiquaire. (Tu trouveras cela)

La fleur est toujours dans l'amande. Par cette admirable devise voilà la maison, voilà la chambre signées d'une intimité inoubliable etc....... Ainsi la maison de Bosco va de la terre au ciel Elle a la verticalité de la tour s'élevant des plus terrestres et aquatiques profondeurs jusqu'à la demeure d'une âme croyant au ciel. Une telle maison est vraiment complète Elle fait la charité d'une tour à ceux qui peut-être n'ont même pas connu un colombier.

—

On doit définir un homme par l'ensemble des tendances qui le poussent à dépasser l'humaine condition

—

Les objets gardés dans le "chosier", dans cet étroit musée des choses qu'on a aimées, sont des talismans de rêveries.

Bachelard. (ta maison;
2° être, chalet)

La Terre et les Rêveries de la Volonté.

Les objets de la Terre nous rendent l'écho de notre
promesse d'énergie. Le travail de la matière
dès que nous lui rendons tout son onirisme,
éveille en nous un narcissisme de notre courage.

L'image est toujours une promotion de l'Être.
Il y a un temps du granit.... la nature possède
un psychochronos, un temps de feu....
Déjà la sensation tactile qui fouille la substance,
prépare l'illusion de toucher le fond de la matière.
L'instinct a toujours à sa disposition une volonté
incisive. Notre vie est remplie de ces expériences curieuses
que nous taisons et qui reviennent en notre inconscient
de rêveries sans fin. Qu'on songe à la fente nette et
frémissante d'une gelée traversée par le couteau, à elle chair
qui ne saigne pas....
La pâte: équilibre entre eau et terre. — dynamique du
poing fermé sans violence et sans mollesse: rêve manuel;
"tout m'est pâte, je suis pâte à moi-même." Il nous faut
comprendre que la main aussi bien que le regard, a ses rêveries
et sa poésie. Nous devons donc découvrir les poèmes du
toucher, les poèmes de la main qui pétrit. —
Une pâte malheureuse suffit à donner à un homme malheureux
la conscience de son malheur.

Le visqueux. Il est amusant de constater que celui qui a
peur d'une matière visqueuse s'en met partout.
S'il me fallait à toute force vivre le gluant, c'est moi-même
qui serait glu. J'irais tendre des gluaux dans le buisson,
poussant dans le pipeau des chants d'hypocrisie!

Toute créature doit surmonter une anxiété. Créer, c'est
dénouer une angoisse. Il y a une sorte d'asthme de
travail au seuil de tout apprentissage.
La simplicité est archaïque. Il faut avoir vécu dans un
vieux jardin pour dire avec foi toutes les vertus du lys
et de l'arnica. Alors la substance est un songe de jeunesse,
la substance est une maladie consolée, une santé parlée.

«Je mets une pomme sur la table, [...] puis je me mets dans cette pomme. Quelle tranquillité.» Tout rêveur que le voudra, ira miniaturisé habiter la pomme. On peut énoncer comme un postulat de l'imagination: les choses rêvées ne gardent jamais leurs dimensions. La plus grande lutte ne se fait contre les forces imaginées. Elle se fait contre les forces imaginées. L'homme est un drame de symboles ⊙

Qu'est-ce le vin? Un corps vivant où se tiennent en équilibre les x esprits ⊙ les plus divers, les esprits volants et les esprits pondérés, conjonction d'un ciel et d'un terroir. Mieux que tout autre végétal la vigne trouve l'accord des mercures de la terre donnant ainsi au vin son juste poids. Elle travaille tout le long de l'année en suivant la marche du soleil à travers tous les signes zodiacaux. Le vin n'oublit jamais, au plus profond des caves, de recommencer cette marche du soleil dans les maisons c'est en marquant ainsi les saisons qu'il trouve le plus étonnant des arts: l'art de vieillir — D'une matière toute substancielle, la vigne prend à la lune, au soleil, à l'étoile un peu de soufre pur seul capable de bien «élémenter» tous les feux des vivants. Le vin est vraiment un universel qui sait se rendre singulier. ⊙

P. S. — Carissimo fratello Alan: Il est temps que je cesse de copier — à défaut d'un œil. Sûr d'être compris à travers et moyennant ce sublime Bachelard, je ose espérer que tu le recevras avec le même enthousiasme et l'étonnement qui a été capable de s'alimenter les moments les plus assombris de mes faiblesses.— En échange, je désire vivement de connaître ton étonnement.— En parenthèse: Le COMBLE du Comble: Il a été scientifique nucléaire, froidement cela!!! Quel re-virement.

Each New Year, I'd send them a nice calendar.
Bit by bit, Vera got sicker and sicker.
Toward the end of August 1987, I got this note:

Gerardo & Vera Muench

"She died on August 1 after long, nightmarish months of dementia.
Why did we lose touch? I miss you so much.
What did I do? No recollection.
Maybe all of this is an illusion. I'm almost blind despite the operation.
The rest not worth mentioning.
I'm waiting
Gerhart,
With deep friendship"

I mailed the last calendar, a calendar in the Occitan language, for New Year's 1988. This is the answer that came. The writing slants upward—typical of a person who is about to die.

Apartado 23 - 61500 - Zitácuaro, Michoacán (México) - Tel: (91-725) 6 06 26

"Dear Alan, my brother,
I've had a relapse, almost blind,
can't answer you, but I received your friendship.
Forgive me—I'm crushed.
Completely abandoned—afraid I'll die soon
That's all
Forgive your G"

I didn't get anything else after that.

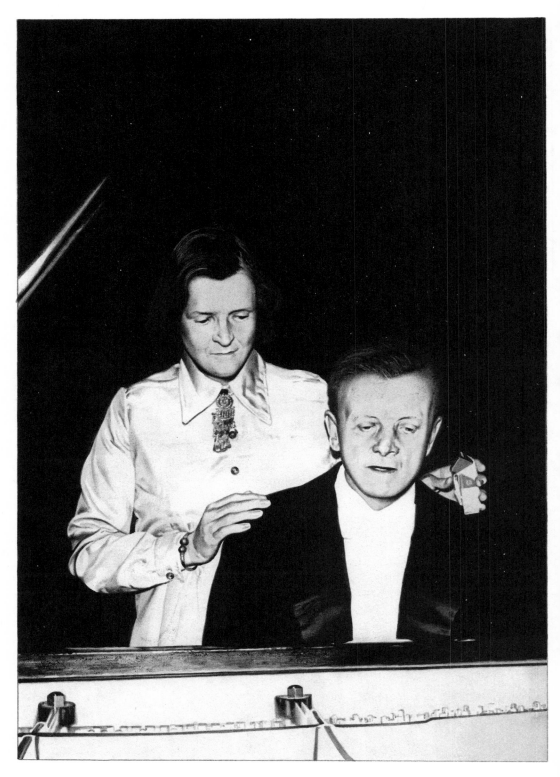

39

You may recall that I had met Gerhart and Vera in Bad Wiessee, when I was with a private by the name of Jim Post.

As luck would have it, when I was getting back in touch with them, in 1979, I was reading that famous book by Truman Capote, "In Cold Blood." It's the story of two criminals murdering a family in late 1950s Kansas. During their trial, Truman Capote mentions the name of the chaplain of the prison where they were being held: Reverend James E. Post.

It's a true story, you know? Not a novel. The names are real.

Jim, like me, had wanted to be a minister. He was from Kansas. It would've been just like him to become a prison chaplain. I said to myself: that could well be him.

I wrote to the book's editor, in America, asking him to kindly forward the enclosed envelope, which I'd left unsealed, to the Reverend James E. Post.

He did, and I got an answer.

It was indeed my Jim Post.
He was pleased to hear from me and sent
me writings he was using in his work
as chaplain.
He'd go from town to town and from
prison to prison, giving talks for a program
called "Save Our Boys," or "Save Our
Children," I can't remember which.
The implication was, save them from
delinquency or jail.
The goal was to persuade parents that
when their children show the warning
signs of antisocial, i.e. criminal, behavior,
something has to be done through
the Christian Protestant religion.
It was basically a very good idea,
but it sounded so fundamentalist
that it didn't thrill me.

I personally did a lot of work
with juvenile delinquents in prison;
it was a large part of my life.
So I was in total agreement
with the initiative, but not so much
with the method.
Not everyone can love Christ that way.
If religion is used simply as a means of
saving a child, it becomes hypocrisy.
As a parent, if you're preaching what
you don't believe in, that's no good. He
also told me about the death of Chaplain
Elliot, in a tone that irked me:
"Dear, dear Chaplain Elliot is dead..."
Europeans don't know what Protestant
fundamentalism is like in the U.S., because
there's nothing like it in Europe.
It's unbearable. It literally oozes saccharine
sentimentality.

It wasn't surprising that Jim would
put some religious preconditions
on renewing our friendship.
In '46, when we spent time together,
I thought like he did, and we both
wanted to do the same work.
He couldn't have imagined
that I'd changed.
I told him. I wrote him that I was
very happy to have found him—it
was true, I liked him—but that I
couldn't renew our friendship on
such religious grounds.
Plus I blamed so-called Christianity
for a good number of the evils
of the modern world.
I never considered the Christian church
to be the church of Jesus.
The Christian church was founded
not by Jesus, or Peter, or any
of the Apostles, but by Paul.
And Paul was at core a moralizing
and anti-erotic misogynist.
Read the Bible; you'll see.

Okay, I guess my letter
was somewhat cruel.
I was probably wrong.
In my life I've often been wrong.
But I was honest, and I wanted to
renew our friendship on a basis
of total frankness.

In any event, he never answered me.

Thanks to some lucky breaks, and often, a lot of effort, I was able to find almost all my friends, one by one.
I found Egypt, but that fits in better with my teenage memories.
We'll talk about that elsewhere.

She told me that Patzi, my first fiancée, had died in an accident.

Through Egypt I found Flint.
He and I have had a lengthy correspondence, with some sharp disagreements on religion, but without being driven apart.
We write each other every Christmas.

I found Dominique d'Antona thanks to the general delivery system. I remembered that after the war he had married the daughter of a prominent hardware store owner in Fort Smith, Arkansas.
I wrote to him there.
A few weeks later, my phone rang.
It was him. He told me:
"I've had a wonderful life. Five kids, all of them college graduates.
I've made a lot of money."

That's great! Not me.

He added: "Call me as often as you like and reverse the charges. I'll pay."

I wrote two letters, but got no answer.
I was about to call him when I received a note from his son.
Dominique, who'd never had the slightest heart problem, had died suddenly of a heart attack.

I found Lou without really finding him.
I had to go to the ends of the earth to get his address in New Jersey.
I sent letters and photos. No response.
In that case, too, it was his daughter who wrote to me—the daughter whose birth
they were awaiting when I spent a month at their house, in '48.
Sure enough, Lou had built houses his whole life.
His wife had died the year before.
He was suffering from what his family believed to be an ulcer. He never said anything,
brave as always.
He went to Florida with a fellow worker and died there.
His daughter found my opened letter in his papers, a sign that he'd received and read it.
But he never answered me.

She sent me this picture of Lou as an old man.

My stepmother, my father's second
wife, one day admitted to me in a
letter that she'd received a phone
call quite a while ago from a certain
Tina, who was looking for me.
My stepmother, who could be
a real idiot, had told her:
"But you have to leave Alan
alone now; he's married."
I was not only married;
I was already a grandfather!

I had a feeling that this Tina might be
Klementine, little Klementine
Rossbauer from Regensburg,
so I wrote to her cousin Erich,
who still lived there,
to ask for her address.
That's how I got back in touch
with Erich, who I call
"my brother Erich" and
occasionally write to.
He gave me an address somewhere
in the Michigan boondocks, and
that's how I found Klementine.

She had married an American soldier
who brought her to America.
He's dead now.
She has two children
and makes a living playing the organ
in clubs, churches, and so on.
She sent me a picture and a small
record she'd made with her son
accompanying her on the drums.
I'll play it for you.
Just hearing her voice and seeing her
face at 50 years of age,
you'll be able to visualize how sweet
she was at 16.
Very simple, fresh-faced,
and talented.
She took a stage name, Tina Zenta,
using her middle name.

We don't write very often,
but when we do, it's interesting,
and fairly personal.
I have to write to her
in the next few days.

Finally, I'm going to talk about Landis.
He had come to see me in France shortly
after my first marriage, because some of his
relatives were French, and he was visiting them.
He was with his father and both of them took
the opportunity to go to Bavaria,
which I'd described to them in glowing terms.
He brought me back a pair of lederhosen,
those famous leather shorts with suspenders.
They were two sizes too big, but I altered them.
They were the ones I was wearing the day
I went to see Crommelynck.

I was invited to visit Landis's
family in Paris. They were
very upper-crust, and I
showed up in my lederhosen.
They were a bit surprised,
but why shouldn't I have?
He'd given them to me.

My French wasn't very good yet. I remember them
correcting me:

Would you like some cheese, sir?

Oh, sure, un petit bout (a little chunk).

It's incorrect to say "bout;" you have to say "morceau" (piece).

We walked all around Paris, Landis, my wife, and I.
He was thrilled because there were street
urchins everywhere.
Landis had read a lot, as I told you, and in all those stories
about the old Paris there were always street urchins.
Landis exclaimed:

Finally! I've seen street urchins!

Later he sent me some
very nice poems,
impeccably typed.
I can't find
them anywhere;
I must have lost them.
They were really good.
Even at 18 his poems
were already good.

He settled in San Francisco.
He wrote me from there to explain that
he'd been raped and had liked it a lot.
I wasn't surprised or angry.
We wrote each other fraternal, intimate
letters in those years of the mid-50s.
Then I got divorced and we stopped writing
to each other.

When I felt the urge to reconnect with my
friends, I looked for Landis too, of course.
I wrote to the Coronado address more than
once, and finally a woman answered me:
"We bought those people's house, I don't
know where they are, but I think they're
all dead."
Ah, darn! I thought.
For a while I believed it.
And then one day I rejected that idea
and called overseas information.
It worked incredibly fast, and I soon got
Landis on the phone, in San Francisco.

I was over 60, and he was close to that
himself. He was pleased and surprised.

How are you?
Are you married?

–"Oh no, no.
I'm still gay."

I wrote to Coronado and I was told
you were all dead. A woman told me.

–"Wow! Really? She
said that? My parents are
dead, but my brother and
I are still here."

We decided to start corresponding again. In a letter I asked him to send me a copy of "Pisan Canto 75," Ezra Pound's poem devoted to Gerhart; I was looking for it at the time. I thought it would be easy for a man like Landis, who was surrounded by books. He didn't respond. Finally I called him.

Did you find the poem I asked you about?

— "No, I didn't."

Excuse me for asking, but why not?

—"It's too tiring."

His voice was sort of strange.

Your voice is kind of funny, what's wrong?

— "Nothing. I'm sick."

— "The flu."

There was a pause, as if he were trying to specify his illness.

There was no news after that. He didn't answer my phone calls. Finally, he wasn't listed in the phone book any more. They were starting to talk about AIDS at the time, and I figured he'd probably contracted it.

That's Landis's story, and it's so sad that it ended that way.

301

40

What should we call my war story?
Pygmies have a tradition I like.
They gather around a storyteller and yell out topics.

For instance, when someone in the group says "Love!" the storyteller responds:
"Love? It's like this." Or: "Hate!" "Hate? It's like this."
And then he develops his story.

You could call my story:
"War? It's like this."

But you can do
as you wish.

One last anecdote.

When I arrived at the École des Métiers
d'Art, in Paris, right after the war,
they had a hazing—
a fairly decent and entertaining one.

They made us dress up as prehistoric
men and women.
Everybody was smeared with paint,
boys and girls alike, and covered
with the kinds of things easily
found in an art school.
It's strange, but I don't remember what
I had to wear.

Most of all I remember
(and it was pretty funny)
that they gave each of us
a Metro ticket and told us
to get on the train at St. Paul,
on the Neuilly-Vincennes line,
and make a particular trip.
I can't remember how long it took,
but I recall that we had to change trains
at least once.

We were carrying giant fake clubs
and huge knives covered with aluminum
foil, and we had to terrify our
fellow passengers, screaming and
shouting as we ran through the
corridors of the Metro.

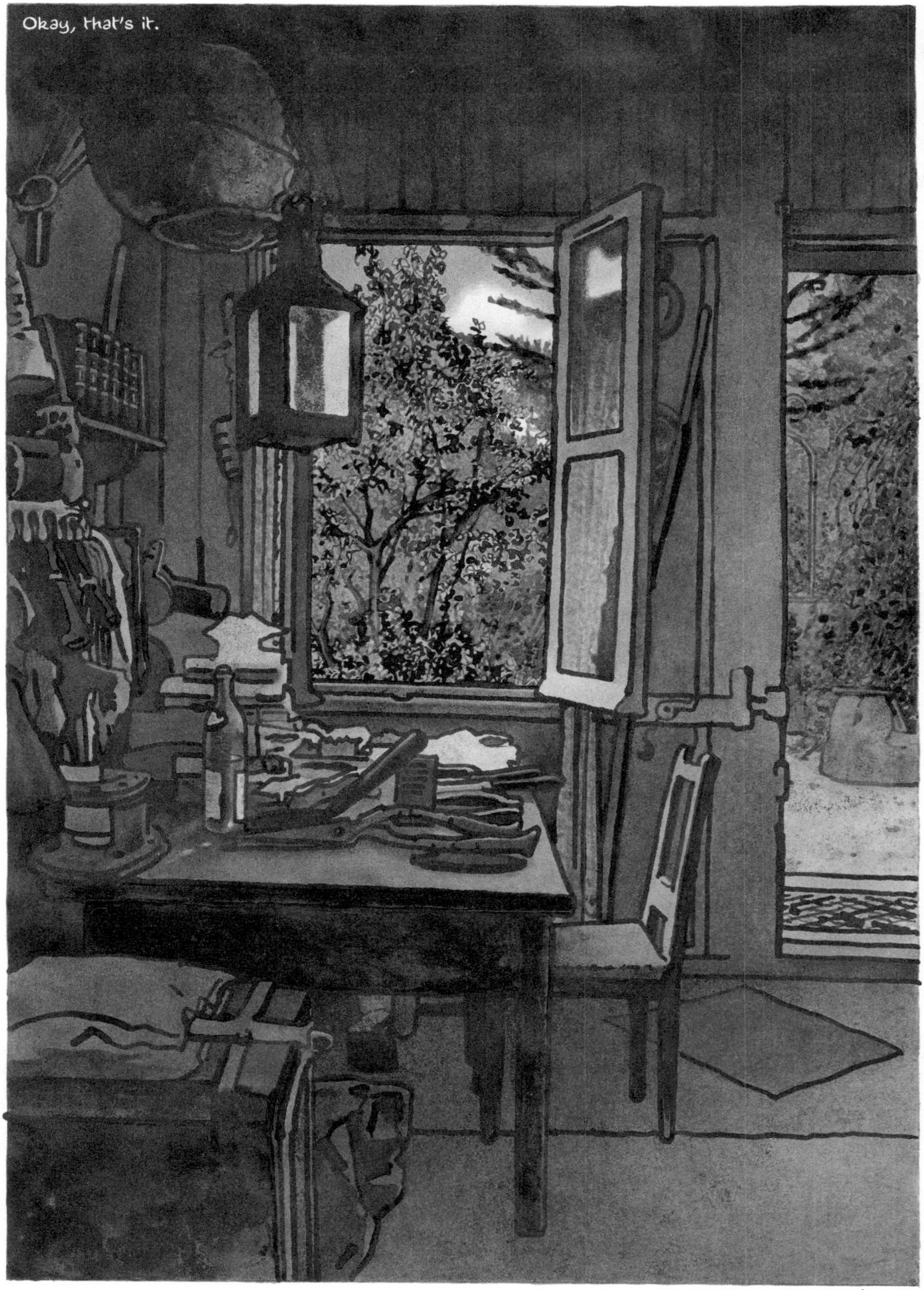
Okay, that's it.

PHOTOGRAPHIC
MEMORIES

Fort Knox

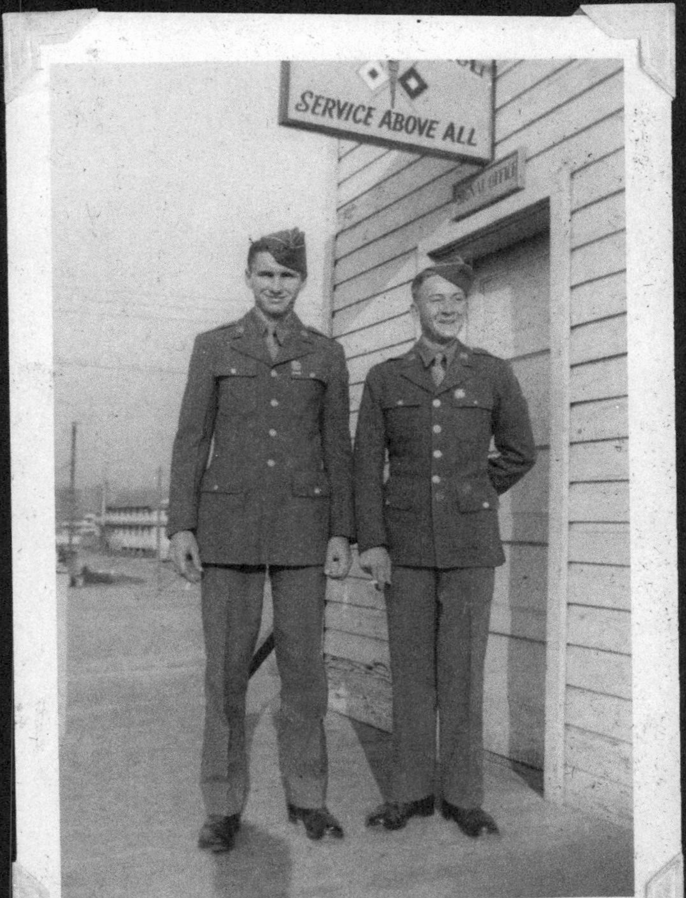
SERVICE ABOVE ALL

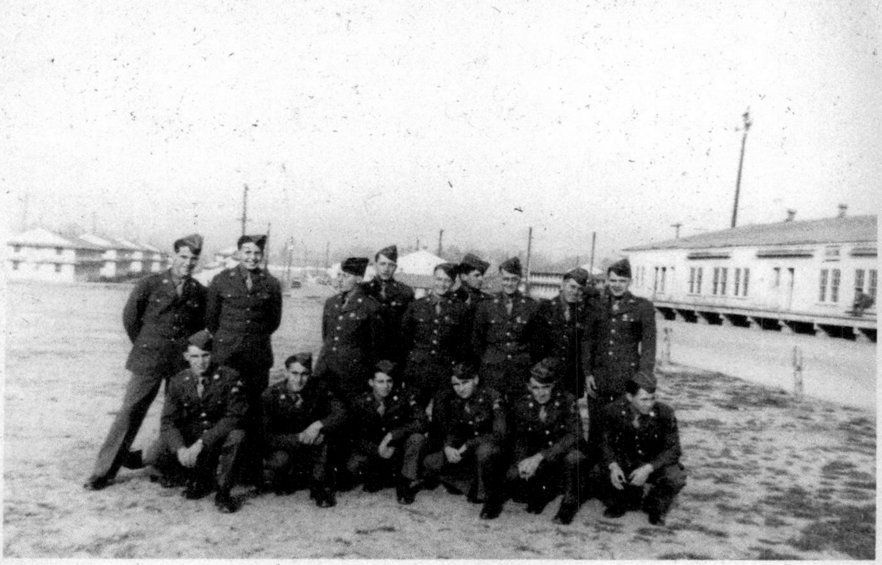

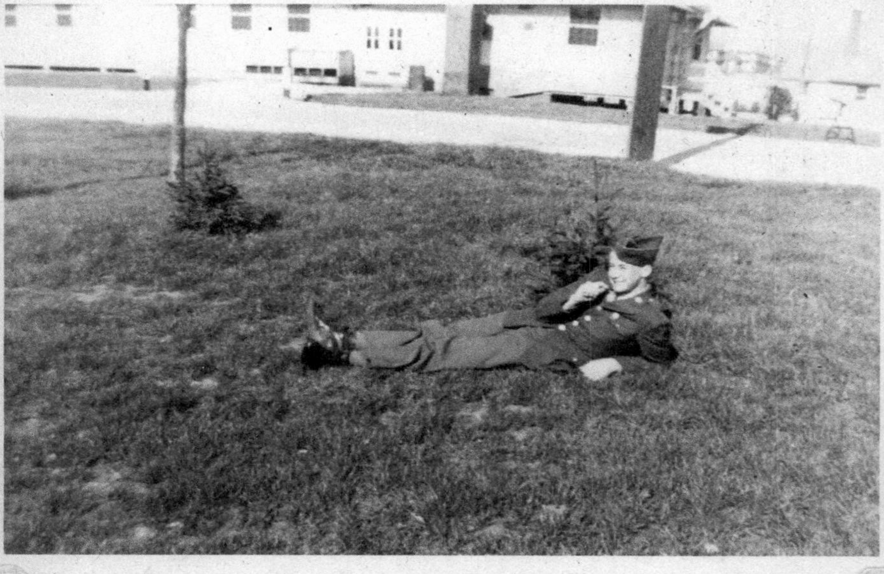

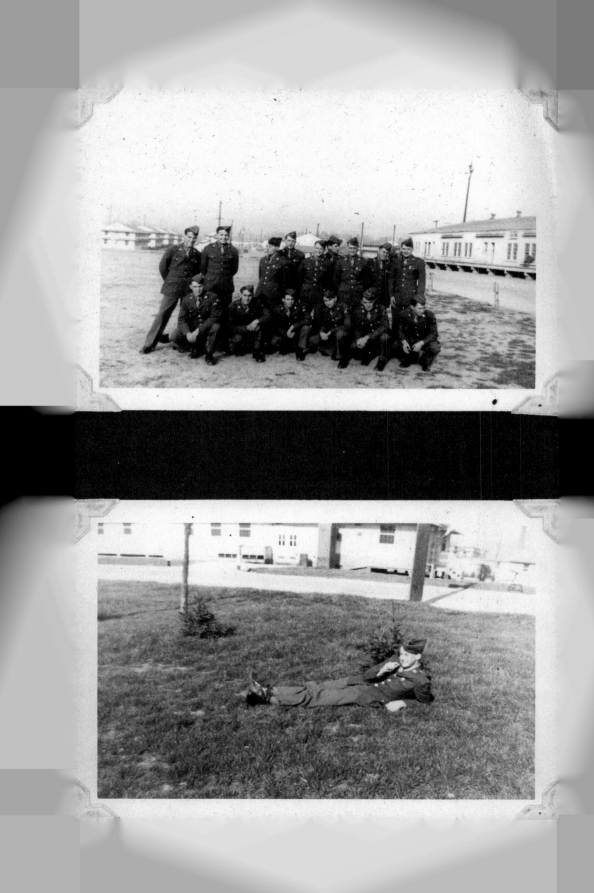

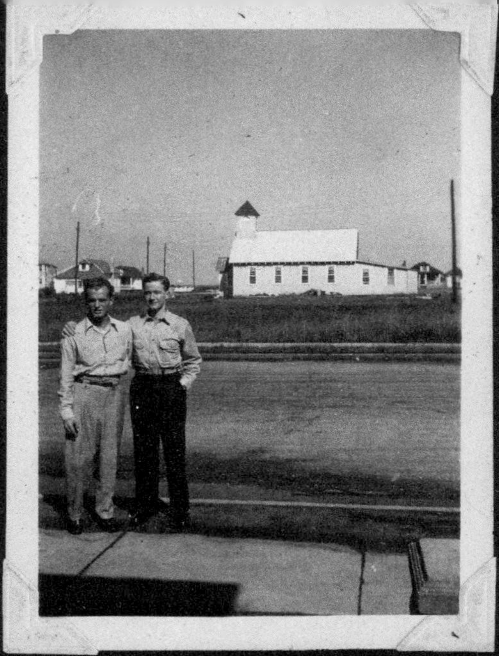

Lou

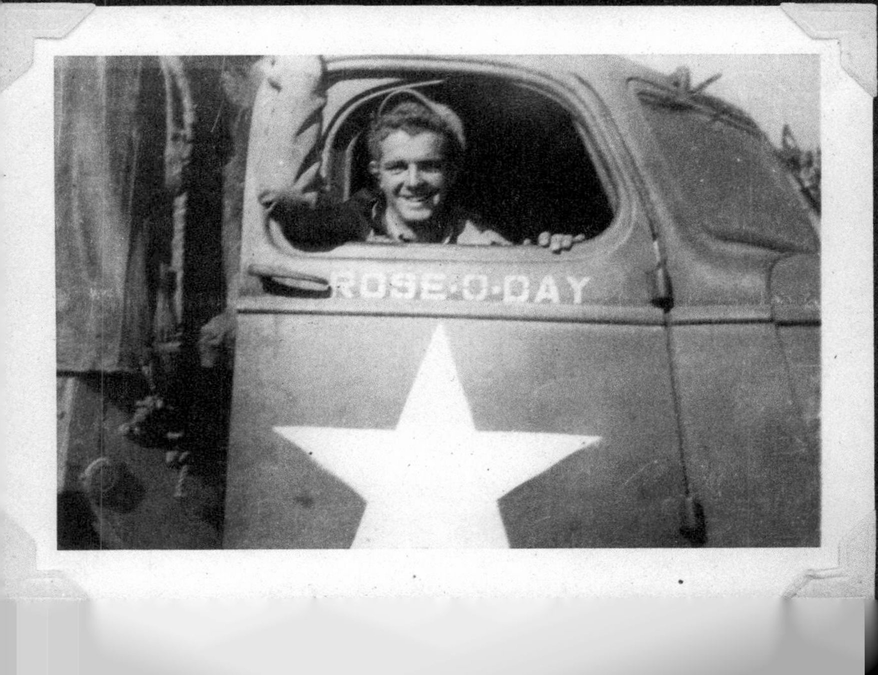
ROSE-O-DAY

A corporal who isn't Cope
shaking the hand of a general
who isn't Patton

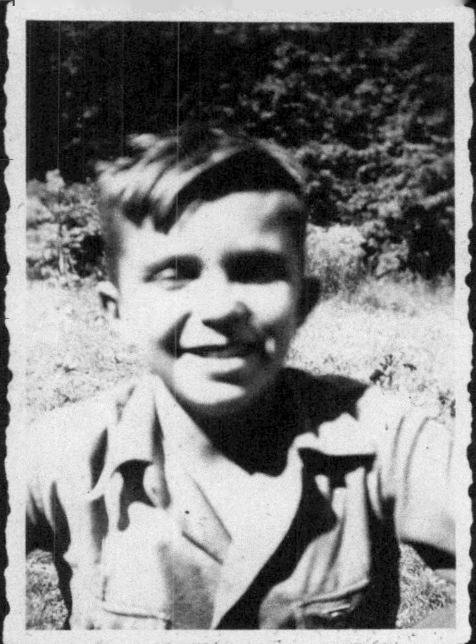
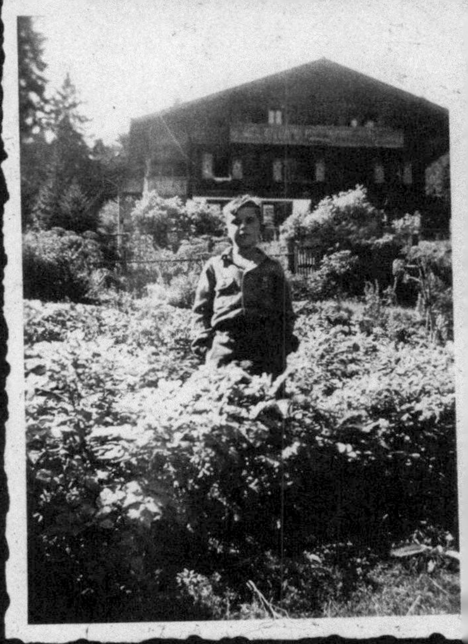

JAKO (Bohemia, 1945)

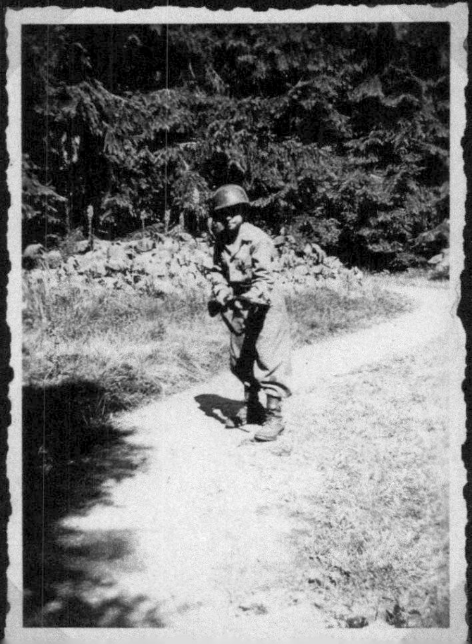
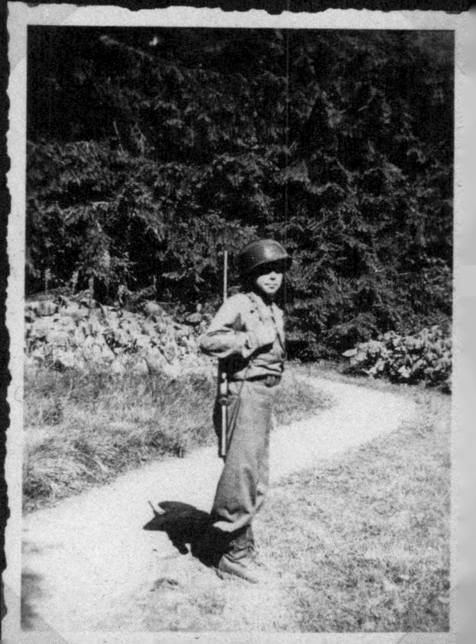

Regensburg. The Rossbauer family

Alan. Klementine. Uncle Peppi. Hans. Anna

Anna   Alan

Klementine. Alan. Erich

Bad Wiessee
am Tegernsee

Hotel Askania

With Klementine's
jacquard sweater

With the civilian
employee's uniform

USA 1947

Redlands

The hike with the Mexican kids

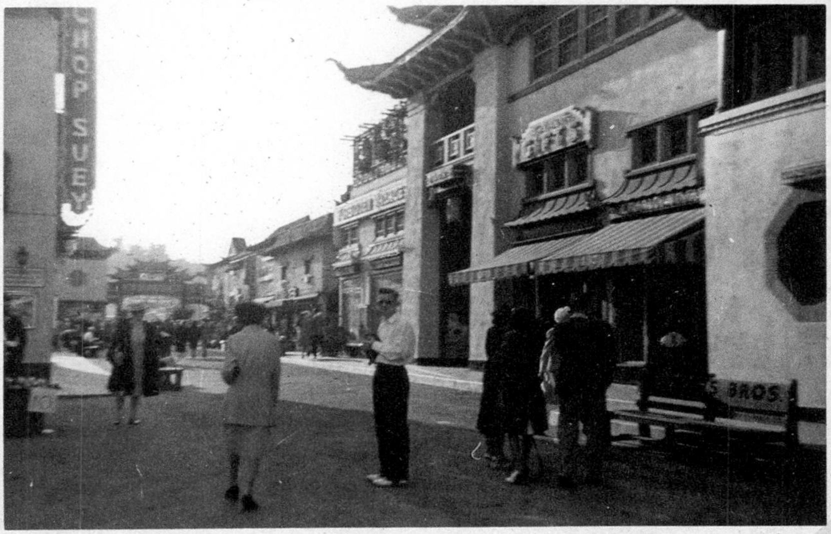
CHOP SUEY
BROS.

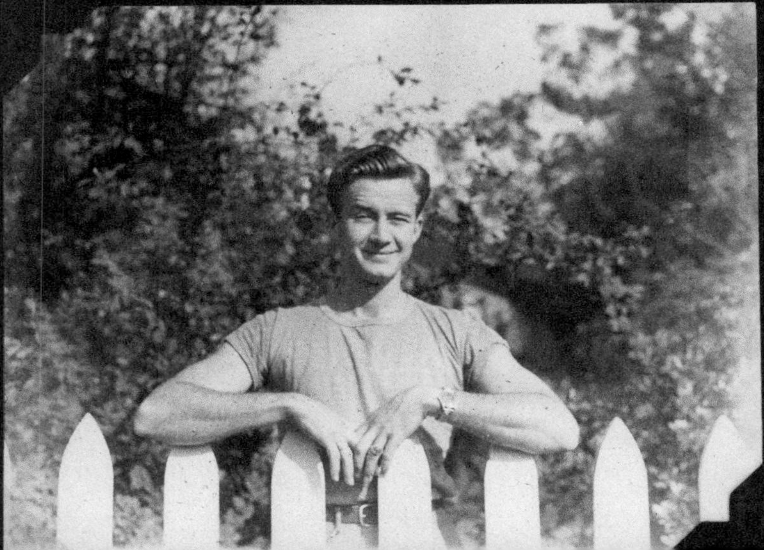

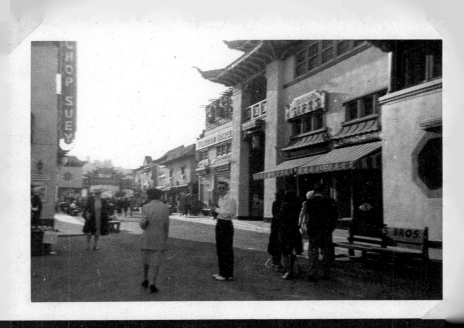

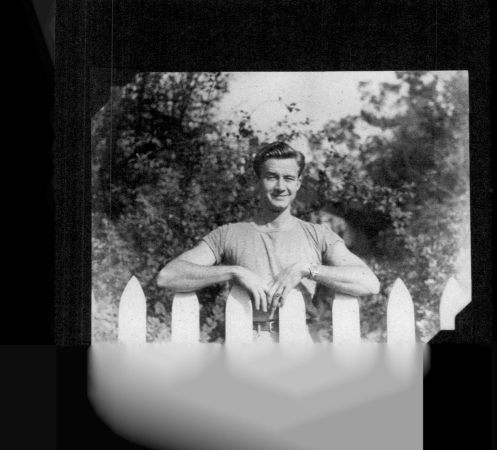

Paris 1949. Hôtel Salé

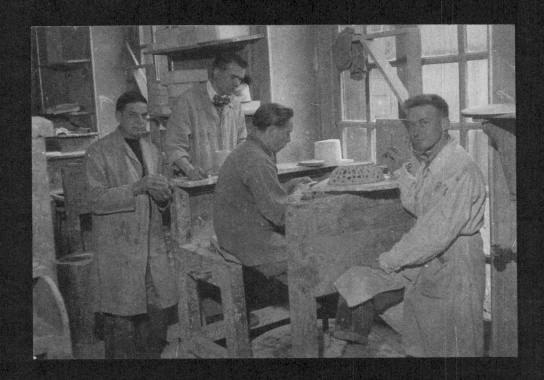

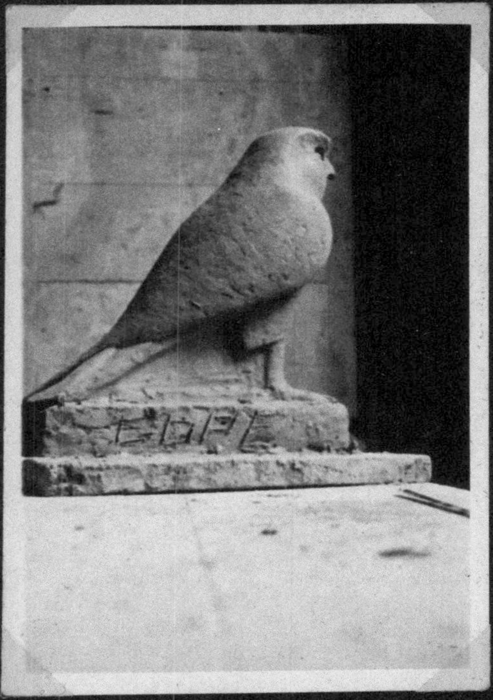

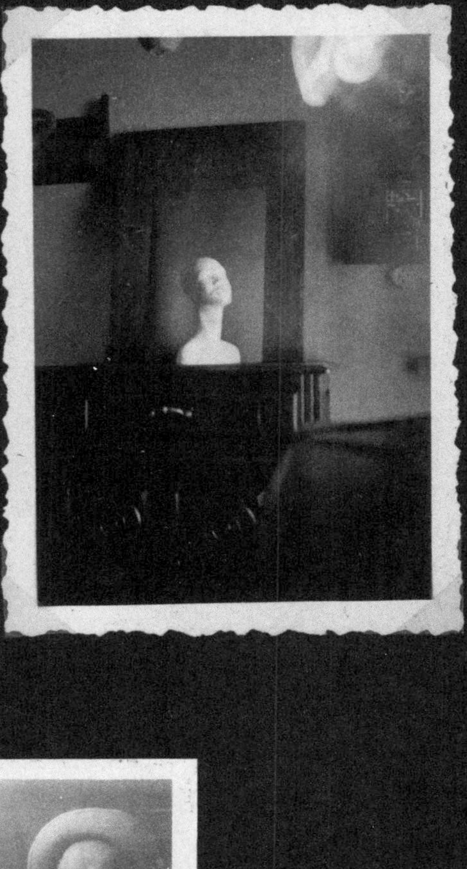

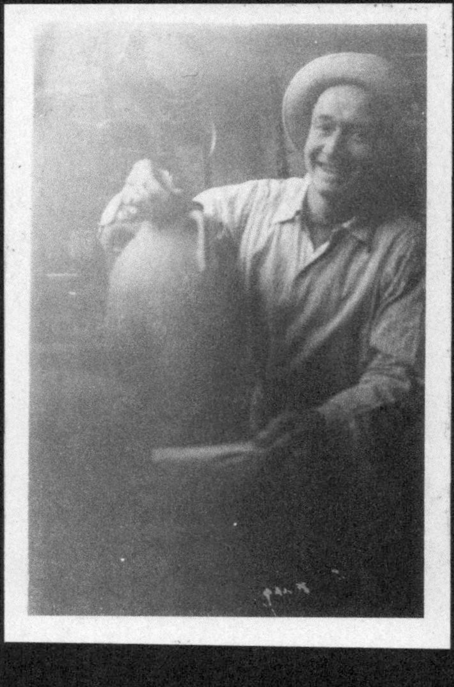

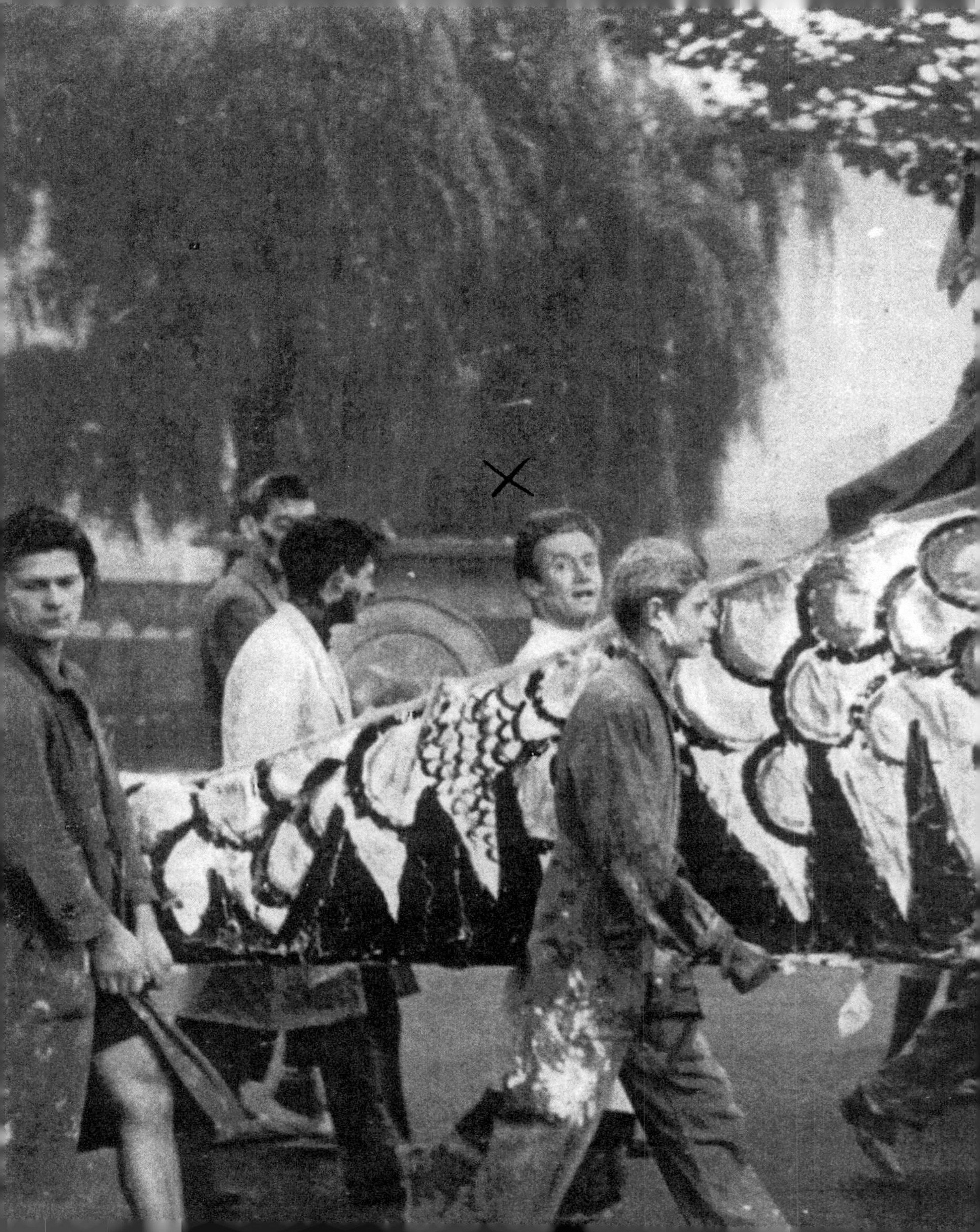

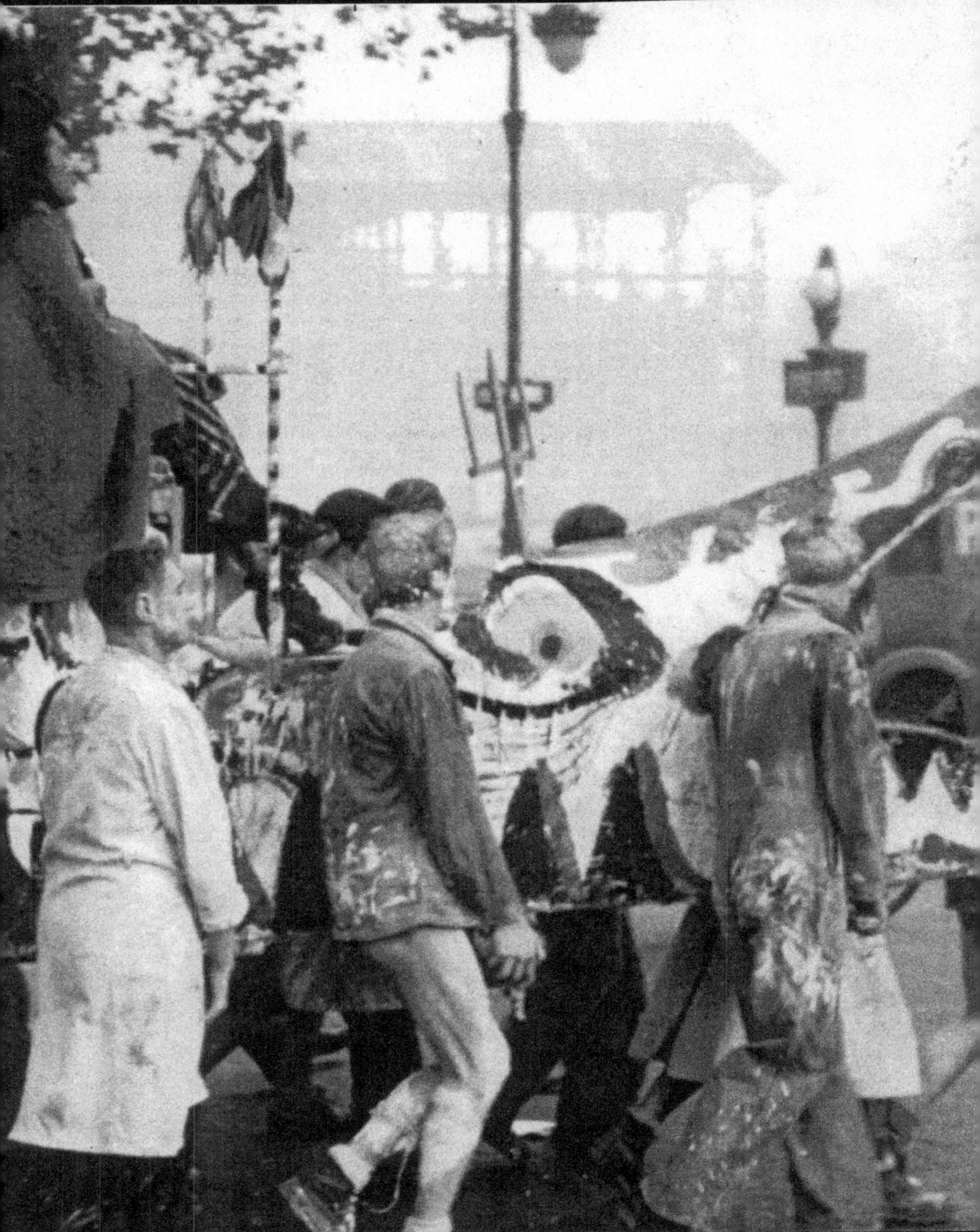

The hazing

Thank you to Klementine and her children.

Thank you to Erich and to the Rossbauer family for welcoming me in Regensburg,
just like they had welcomed Alan sixty years earlier. Thanks to them, I was able to cross
the threshold of the home on 1, Cow Lane, pace around Hans's tiny garden, and go down
into Anna's cellar.

Thank you to Lothar Erett for his contribution to these meetings.

Thank you to Bernhard Kaiser for reserving me a room with a balcony overlooking Lake
Tegernsee at his Askania Hotel in Bad Wiessee, and for giving me access to his archives.

Thank you to Leni and Gisela for sharing their memories of 1945-1946.

Thank you to Mario Beauregard for the photograph of Gerhart and Vera,
from *Plural* magazine (Mexico City, January 1978).

Thank you to Thierry Garrel and Peter Fleischmann for the images of the Palatinate region
contained in their remarkable documentary *Mon ami l'assassin* (*My Friend the Murderer*)
(Fufoofilm-Arte 2006).

Thank you to Bill, Maria and Panchito for lending their home in Pasadena,
which was an ideal base camp on the road to the giant sequoias.

Warm greetings to Vance, from Ventura, and Thierry Mallet, from Venice.

Thank you to Mado and Claude Perrault, Liliane and André Perrier,
Suzanne and Henry Burel for the pleasant hours we spent together on the island.

Hi to Jacqueline Chazelas, to Madeleine Audouys, to Monique and Christophe,
to the Kerebels, the Shears, the Signorellos, to Pierre Soler.

A toast for Lucienne. Another for Yves, Ursula, Sophie and Benoît.

Thank you to Lila and Jérémi Marissal for having preceded me in old Regensburg
and having sent a few pictures, as my scouting party.

Thank you to Pierre and Françoise Lèbe.

Thank you to Jed Falby for his "rumble seat" and his camaraderie.

Thank you to Frédéric Lemercier for his amazing Hollywood manor houses,
to François Calame for his rustic log cabins and to Xavier Dandoy de Casabianca
for his beautiful gray Danube.

Thank you to Didier Lefèvre for introducing me to the photographs of Weegee
and to those of Louis Faurer.

Thank you to Mark Siegel and to the team at First Second.

Thank you to Jean-Christophe Menu and to all those who contributed to producing
these books at L'ASSOCIATION.

Thank you to Donatella and Cecilia for their sweet company in California and in Bavaria,
as we walked in Alan's footsteps.